SAARBRUCK TO SEDAN:
THE FRANCO-GERMAN
WAR 1870-1871 VOLUME 1

Saarbruck To Sedan: The Franco-German War 1870-1871 Volume 1

Uniforms, Organisation and Weapons of the Armies of the Imperial Phase of the War

Ralph Weaver

Helion & Company

Helion & Company Limited
Unit 8 Amherst Business Centre
Budbrooke Road
Warwick
CV34 5WE
England
Tel. 01926 499 619
Email: info@helion.co.uk
Website: www.helion.co.uk
Twitter: @helionbooks
Visit our blog at blog.helion.co.uk

Published by Helion & Company 2021
Designed and typeset by Mary Woolley (www.battlefield-design.co.uk)
Cover designed by Paul Hewitt, Battlefield Design (www.battlefield-design.co.uk)

Text and colour figures © Ralph Weaver 2021
All other images from the author's collection unless otherwise stated
Maps drawn by George Anderson © Helion & Company 2021

ISBN 978-1-914059-88-9

British Library Cataloguing-in-Publication Data.
A catalogue record for this book is available from the British Library.

For details of other military history titles published by Helion & Company Limited contact the
above address or visit our website: http://www.helion.co.uk.

We always welcome receiving book proposals from prospective authors.

Contents

Preface

The war of 1870–1871 has been variously referred to as the 'Franco–Prussian War' or the 'Franco–German War'. Although Prussia was the largest state and leading political power in Germany, France faced the armed forces of all the German states, the North German Confederation of Prussia and the smaller states who mostly fought on the side of Prussia in 1866 and those kingdoms south of the river Main who had been Prussia's foes in that conflict. For this reason, the series has the title of 'The Franco–German War'. Interestingly, most French sources refer to the period as 'The War of 1870', no doubt to distinguish it from the other Franco–German wars of the preceding centuries.

Names used in the text are generally given in their anglicised form except where the native name is well known and accepted. Where appropriate, measurements are given using the metric system with an imperial equivalent in brackets. Use of the German mile (geographical mile) where quoted from original sources has been converted to metric and imperial figures: 7.4 kilometres (4.6 US and British miles). Occasionally the term 'league' turns up in old texts, this unit was based on how far a person could walk in an hour: 3 miles/5½ kilometres. A useful concept as not only did it indicate distance, but also the time it would take to get there.

This book is not an historical account of the Franco–German War, but a detailed look at the armies, the men and their generals, how they fought, what weapons they used and what uniforms they wore. Up to 1870 soldiers could be distinguished by their uniforms, the colour of their tunics, the badges and plumes on their headgear, the designs on their flags and standards and the shapes of their hats. After 1871, and in some countries before, military leaders had planned and experimented with uniforms that blended in with the soldier's environment. Browns, greys, black and green were in use until the twentieth century when camouflage was opted for and the visual presence of the soldier all but disappeared from the battlefield. Finances permitting, brightly coloured uniforms were now reserved for the parade ground.

Introduction

On 26 July 1866 the Peace of Nikolsburg, later ratified by the Treaty of Prague, brought an end to hostilities between Austria and Prussia. Prussia took its share of the spoils diplomatically letting Austria off lightly with a small indemnity, but most importantly, excluding her from any political influence in the old German Confederation that she had dominated for the previous 50 years.

The Austro–Prussian War was the second war (the first was against Denmark in 1864) engineered and used by Prussia's leading minister, Otto von Bismarck, in his avowed aim to bring all Germany under the sway of the Prussian monarchy. The Battle of Königgrätz in Bohemia (now Hradec Králové in the Czech Republic), alternatively named after the nearby village of Sadowa, sealed the fate of Austria and was as much a defeat for the French. Napoleon III had counted on the war between the German-speaking states being a long-drawn-out affair giving him the opportunity to intervene and become the peacemaker of Europe and dictate his own terms to the exhausted parties. With Bismarck now in the driving seat in European politics, the French smarted under what they saw as a humiliating situation and many leading figures in France felt that sooner or later war between themselves and Prussia would have to settle the matter of European dominance.

Short though it was, Prussia took notice of its effects on their army and introduced changes to their tactics and equipment. For the Prussians, it was the revelation of the power of artillery; even the Austrian muzzle-loading guns had proved a major factor on the battlefield. The majority of Prussia's old artillery pieces, those which dated from the 1830s, were replaced with the new steel breech-loading guns supplied by the Krupp factory which fired percussion fused ammunition that burst on impact. The Prussian General Staff, in the person of General Moltke, also looked at their battlefield tactics and decided they needed to make some changes to devolve more responsibility to junior officers who, it was realised, actually controlled battlefield tactics. Also, some alterations were made to practical arrangements in deploying artillery, in some cases in the front line, and the use of cavalry in scouting and gathering intelligence and denying similar actions by enemy horsemen.

France also took note of the major aspects of the war, particularly the technical improvements in armaments, and introduced their own breech-loading rifle – the Model 1866, developed by Antoine Alphonse Chassepot – and developed a mechanical machine gun, more properly a 'volley gun' mounted on a field artillery carriage. The French were confident their combat tactics, though developed in North Africa and adapted after service in Crimea (1854), Italy (1860) and Mexico (1863–1867) would be sufficient to defeat the Prussians. Based on their experiences in the field, the French generals were also confident in their abilities and skill.

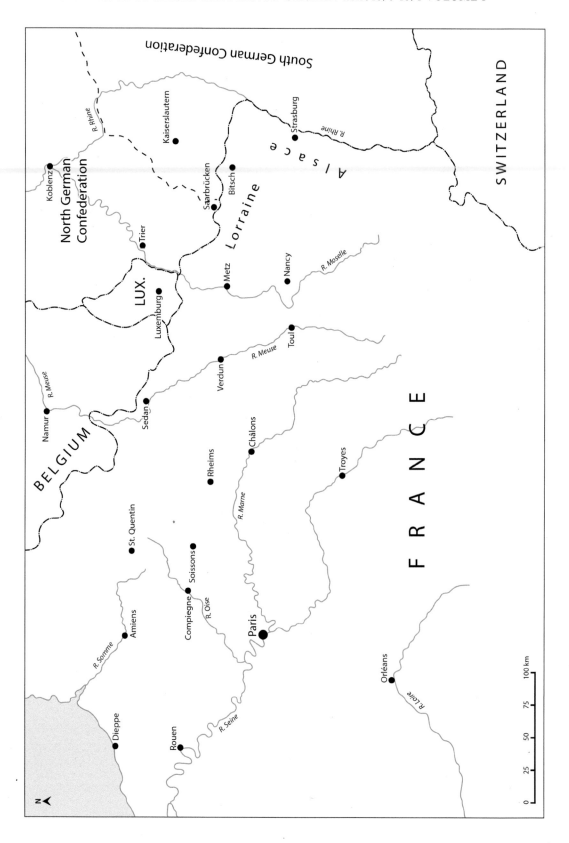

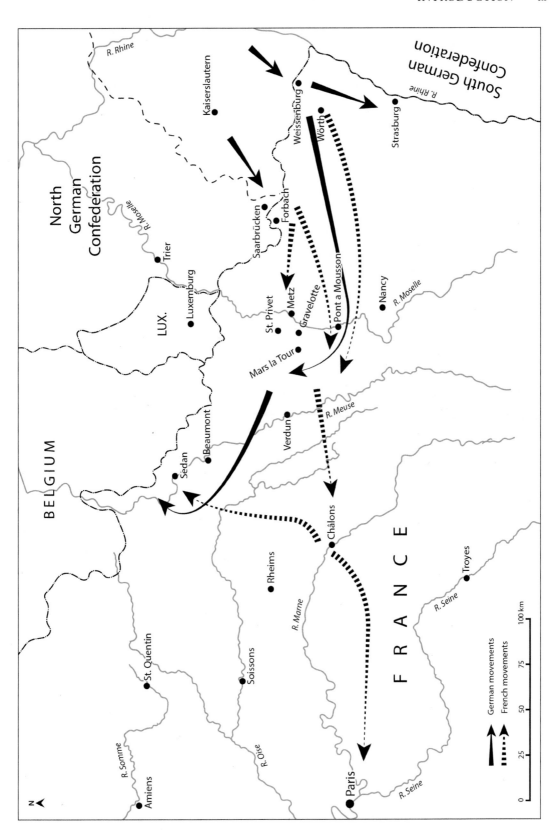

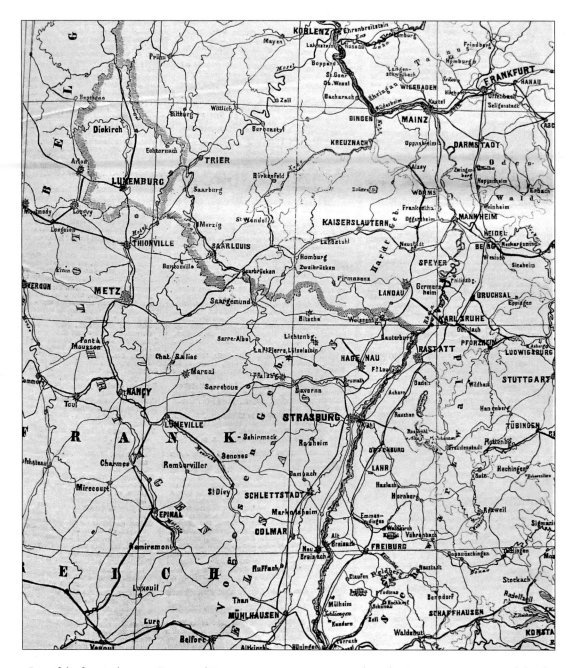

Part of the frontier between France and Prussia, part running east-west where the German armies were mobilised.

1

Imperial Phase: Saarbruck to Sedan

To set the scene, a brief outline of the course of the war will be useful from the declaration of hostilities to the end of empire with the defeat of the French Army at Sedan and the surrender of Napoleon to the Prussian king.

The French Army (or at least its generals) that set out in July 1870 was full of confidence in its abilities to take on the Prussians, invade Germany and, with the help of the south German states, march on to Berlin. (This seemed to be Napoleon's plan in a general sort of way.) After all, the first Napoleon had done just that in October 1806 at the battles of Jena and Auerstadt, both deep in Germany. However, the French Army of 1870 was not the same as the one that had defeated the Prussian and Saxon armies in 1806 and the Prussian Army was certainly not the same as its forebears. Problems that had been overcome in 1806 proved insurmountable in 1870 and the French Army barely reached the frontiers of Germany before supply systems broke down, reserves wandered the countryside in vain searching for their parent units, and indecision and lack of any coherent detailed plan – other than that in the mind of Napoleon, which was to advance across the Rhine around Strasburg – drove corps commanders to despair and left troops with low morale. By the outbreak of the war Napoleon III was a sick man, physically ill, the result of painful bladder stones. After the Battle of Saarbrucken, he had to be lifted from his horse by General Lebrun and Marshall Lebœuf and assisted to a carriage. He was also painfully aware of his limitations as a military leader and gave over command of the French forces in Alsace to Marshall MacMahon.

On the other side of the hill (in this case the Vosges Mountains) the Prussians and their south German allies marched to a plan conceived and continually revised by the Prussian General Staff under the direction of General Moltke, the victor of the War of 1866 and the chief architect of the Prussian success against Denmark in 1864. His plan seemed deceptively simple: three armies were to cross the frontier between Strasburg and Luxemburg, locate the positions of the French forces and defeat them in battle, and then to march on Paris. However, the actual movement to the frontier by the German armies had been planned in meticulous detail.

Since 1866 the peace of Europe had been shaken by one crisis after another. Bismarck had seen that the unification of Germany under Prussian leadership could not be achieved without removing French influence and if that meant war, the North German Confederation was ready. With the incorporation of the smaller German states into the Prussian system and the alliances with the south German states, Moltke assured Bismarck the army could take on France and win. King Wilhelm took an active part in the command of his armies – after all, he had been a soldier since the wars of the first Napoleon. At 73 he was still active and capable of taking the field. His Chief of Staff was younger at 70, but Moltke was also fit and able to bear the difficulties of the campaign.

On 14 July 1870, France resolved on war. The political situation had been strained for some time, with conditions between Berlin and Paris deteriorating and gleefully manipulated by Bismarck to make it appear the blame for the outbreak of the war lay squarely with the French government. On the following day, the French ordered mobilisation of the army and navy and for the troops to concentrate on the frontier.

Numbers

In any account of the organisation of the armies of 1870 there will be a problem with numbers. All the sources, unless copied from one another, will quote different totals of troops incorporated into the different tactical units. There are several reasons for this. First, regulations laid down the composition of units down to and including company level. These figures have been extrapolated by some to calculate the strengths of larger units, divisions and corps. With Prussian forces this may have been tolerably accurate as the system of calling in reserves and mobilising second- and third-line troops was reasonably efficient. However, for the French this led to wildly inaccurate forecasts; even Napoleon, when he reached the forward concentration point at Metz, was unsure of just how many men were under his command.

The second reason is that reserves had to reach their depots to collect their uniforms and equipment and units by whatever means they could. Road, rail and ultimately on foot, Germany and more especially France were filled with men, horses and wagons trying to join up with their companies, squadrons and batteries. Within Prussia and her allies, reserves were recruited within their regimental districts which meant that they did not have to travel far.

Third, as soon as hostilities commenced casualties reduced unit strengths, and the killed, wounded, missing, sick and those who had fallen out on the line of march could not be instantly replaced. Some French units never achieved their intended compliment as reserves, instead of joining their parent unit, were grouped into new, ad hoc formations termed 'régiments de marche'. Not only men were in short supply, but horses and transport wagons were also wanting.

Officially a battalion of French *chasseurs à pied* had had 938 men, six horses, five mules and three vehicles. An infantry regiment of three battalions had 2,785 men, 19 horses, 14 mules and 11 vehicles. A squadron of cavalry 167 men and 144 horses. A battery of field artillery 154 men with 36 horses. A battery of horse artillery 161 men with 94 horses. And so on, multiplying these numbers for brigades, divisions and corps. As the depots of the regiments were scattered all over France, reserves had to travel from their home towns and villages to the depots to collect their arms and uniforms and field equipment and then find their companies and squadrons. At the

Sectional views of rifles used in the conflict.
Top Prussian Dreyse needle gun, middle French Chassepot, bottom Bavarian Werder.

opening of the campaign many battalions fell short of their compliment of 800+ men and could, in some cases, muster no more than 600 or 700.

The regimental history of the 5th Chasseurs à Pied illustrates the problem with the strength of the battalion and the vagaries of the politicians formulating national policies. The battalion occupied the garrison at Rennes, in Brittany, and received the order to mobilise on 15 July. The destination of the battalion was not known; if an alliance was made with Denmark, the regiments in the west of France were to form an active corps to be embarked on the fleet destined for the shores of the Baltic. The regiments stationed in Brittany that were not ordered to the frontier on the Rhine were to concentrate at either Brest or Cherbourg. This alliance with Denmark never materialised and on 20 July the 5th Chasseurs were ordered to Thionville, on the River Moselle near the frontier with Luxemburg and Prussia, as part of the 2nd Division of the 4th Corps. The battalion strength stood at 585 men, six companies formed the field battalion, and two companies were retained at the depot to receive the reserves. Two days later the field battalion marched to the railway station and boarded the train for Thionville, via Paris, Rheims and Sedan, arriving late afternoon on the 23rd.

Artillery Calibre

A word on calibre as applied to artillery. In 1870 guns were generally referred to as '4-pounder', '6-pounder' or '12-pounder'. This no longer applied to the weight of shot, although this had been the case when guns were muzzle-loading smoothbores firing solid round shot. The ammunition used in, say, a Prussian Krupp 4-pounder breech-loader was no longer round, but elongated and weighed approximately double that of the former round shot. There was a move in Prussia to designate batteries equipped with the 4-pounders as 'light' and those equipped with 6-pounders as 'heavy'. The calibre of a 4-pounder was around 80mm and a 6-pounder, 90mm.

The war winner. Krupp's 4-pounder steel breech loader and limber.

The artillery of both combatants was organised into batteries, the smallest administrative unit, similar to a company in the infantry and a squadron in the cavalry. It was made up of a number of guns, ammunition wagons, artillerymen and horses as well as the paraphernalia need to keep the guns and wagons in working order. However, in action any number of guns brought together for a particular task was also termed a 'battery'. In siege or blockade operations the term 'battery' also applied to earthworks protected by gabions or similar and could consist of any number of artillery pieces.

Maps

The topographical section of the Prussian General Staff had the responsibility of preparing and issuing maps to the Army. Although maps were issued in the campaigns of 1864 in Denmark and 1866 in South Germany and Bohemia, there were never enough for the smaller units. In 1870 the scope of those entitled to receive maps was extended to include commanders of cavalry squadrons, batteries of artillery and half battalions of infantry. Two types of maps were prepared: a 'general' map of the area where they were to operate, and what was termed a 'special' map section relative to the unit's task. These latter were copies of the French General Staff map at a scale of 1:80,000 but brought up to date with the latest roads and railways and the addition of a note of the number of inhabitants of each town and village – vital information when demanding quarters for troops at the end of a day's march. This information was readily available from French official statistics. As the troops moved across France, the relevant sections were printed and distributed. The 'spy' mania which gripped France was heightened when German officers arrived in a town and could demand food and lodging according to its population.

The French *Dépôt de la Guerre* had a similar responsibility and the printing presses in Paris produced enormous quantities of maps of Germany where the French Army was supposed to be operating. However, as events moved so quickly, there was no time to provide maps of those parts of France where the campaign was actually being fought. The French Navy was similarly handicapped, and the fleet at Brest due to operate in the North Sea and the Baltic had no charts of those areas.

Medals

Contemporary paintings from the Franco–German War period of soldiers and officers, supposedly taken from life, will sometimes depict the subject displaying a single medal on his chest, or even occasionally a whole row of awards. This is not the artist's licence or fancy but reflects the normal convention of wearing medals in full dress, as is done today. Unlike today, however, full dress is what the soldier of 1870 went to war dressed in, complete with his awards. Photographs, in the form of *'cartes de visite'*, clearly show the subject and his display of awards. The medals were of two types: those given for participation in a particular war, campaign or even battle; and those given to recognise an act of bravery or an action above and beyond what duty would have demanded.

France

In the French Army campaign medals were awarded for participation in the Italian campaign of 1859, the China expedition of 1860 and the war in Mexico. They were silver medals displaying the bust of Napoleon on the obverse and a list of battles on the reverse. The Italian campaign medal was worn on a white ribbon with six red stripes of which 120,000 were issued. The China medal was suspended from a yellow silk ribbon bearing the Chinese characters for 'Peking' in blue thread and with an issue of 8,000. The Mexico medal was worn on a white ribbon with red and green stripes arranged at a 45-degree angle forming a cross, over which was superimposed a black eagle, its wings spread and holding a green snake in its beak and talons, based on the Mexican coat of arms. Some 38,000 were awarded.

French awards for bravery, or meritorious service consisted of the *Médaille militaire*, a silver medal with a profile of Napoleon, topped by an imperial eagle to which was fitted a ribbon of yellow silk edged green, and the highest award for bravery, the *Légion d'honneur*. This was originally established by Napoleon's illustrious uncle in 1802 and was a white enamel five-pointed star hanging from a plain red ribbon. It was awarded to military and civilian recipients in five classes.

French officers were awarded decorations for service with forces beyond the frontiers of the state – for example, the Pope made several officers knights of the Order of St Gregory, the medal of which was a red enamel cross hung from a gold papal coat of arms suspended round the neck from a red ribbon edged yellow. Over 90,000 French troops served in the Crimea, and they were authorised to wear the British award, which was a silver medal bearing the head of Queen Victoria with a light blue ribbon edged yellow and bars denoting the wearer's participation in individual actions. Former members of the Pontifical Zouaves, who, when they returned to France, were renamed the 'Volunteers of the West', continued to wear their papal medals.

Germany

The Prussian award of the Iron Cross was extended to citizens of all German states and under the empire became an all-German award rather than just being limited to Prussia. It had been awarded for meritorious service during the wars of liberation (against Napoleon I) from 1813. It was not awarded again until reintroduced by King Wilhelm I in 1870. The award was issued in three classes: the Second Class Cross, the First Class Cross and the Grand Cross. The ribbon for the Second Class Cross and Grand Cross was black silk with two white bands. The ribbon colours were reversed, white silk with black bands for the civilian award and for non-combatants such as medical staff.

The order of the Black Eagle was Prussia's highest order of chivalry, founded in 1701, an eight-pointed silver starburst with a black Prussian eagle on the central disc. The Red Eagle award was Prussia's second highest order of chivalry, founded in 1705, but re-founded on a number of occasions. A gold medal of the order was awarded to enlisted men. In 1870 only two officers wore the *Pour le Mérite* medal: Moltke and General von Blumenthal. General von Caprivi was awarded the medal in 1871. It is still awarded by the modern German state as a civilian order of merit for achievements in the arts and sciences.

A number of 1864 crosses were awarded to Prussian troops for actions during the war against Denmark. They were of a similar design, a *cross pattée* (with the arms of the cross

The Prussian, later German award, the Iron Cross, 2nd class, 1st class and Grand Cross.

The Prussian Crown Prince awards
the Iron Cross.

slightly curved) over a laurel wreath with a central disc, on the obverse displaying the King of Prussia's bust and, on the reverse, a Prussian eagle standing on a cannon barrel. The arms of the cross give the date and the action. The medal for taking part in the storming of the Duppel fortifications was white bronze with a ribbon of a central wide blue stripe, bordered with a narrow white stripe on each side and a further border of black with a white edge. Several types exist. The medal for the crossing on the Alsen Sound was similar, but in yellow bronze. A medal for all military personnel was issued with the crowned cyphers of the Prussian and Austrian monarchs, who were allies in 1864, on the obverse and an inscription on the reverse, 'Unser tapffern Kriegern 1864'. It was also issued to ships companies who took part in the naval campaign. The ribbon was black silk with two wide stripes close to the edges, one white and the other yellow.

Three crosses were issued for the 1866 campaign against Austria and her allies, of a similar design to the 1864 cross, except that the royal cypher replaced the king's bust on the obverse, one for the army in Bohemia with on the reverse, 'Konig-gratz' on the upper arm of the cross and the date of the battle, 'den 3' and 'Juli' on the cross bars and '1866' on the lower arm. The second cross was awarded to members of the army who fought in central and south Germany, with an inscription of 'Der Main Armee 1866', which refers to the district of the River Main where the actions took place. The third cross was given to men who took part in the war but were not entitled to the first two. The ribbon was the same for all: black with a double stripe of white and orange on either side of the central black portion.

Prussia also had a system of long-service awards, instituted in 1825, worn on the left breast, below any medals. It was awarded in three classes to enlisted men and non-commissioned officers (though not officers) of the Army and Navy for nine, 15 and 21 year's service. It was a metal plate covered with blue silk with a metal clasp bearing the letters 'F.W. III.'. The lowest award had black edges to the ribbon and the clasp was of blackened iron; the next highest had white edging and a clasp of silver; and the highest had yellow edging and a clasp of silver gilt. Members of the *Landwehr* had a long-service decoration of blue silk within a metal frame and with the letters 'F.W.IV.' set between two *Landwehr* crosses all in yellow embroidery. Officers had a single long-service medal awarded after 25 years' service. It was a straight-armed cross of copper gilt with a central disc having a crown under which the letters 'F.W. III.' on the obverse and the Roman characters 'XXV.' on the reverse. It was worn on a plain blue ribbon.

Many soldiers who took part in the Franco–German War had previously served in other German states and been given awards for the 1866 campaign. Former Hanoverian soldiers were entitled to the Langensalza Medal, a bronze medal with a bust of King George V of Hanover on the obverse and the date of the Battle of Langensalza on the reverse, with the words '*LANGENSALZA/27 JUNI/1866*' within a laurel wreath. The ribbon was white with a broad yellow stripe near each edge. Medals were presented to 16,000 former Hanoverian officers and soldiers. The King of Prussia specifically decreed that the medal was to be worn by his former enemies as a gesture of reconciliation.

The small state of Nassau was absorbed into Prussia after 1866, and the last sovereign, Duke Adolph, awarded the '*Feldzeichen fur 1866*' to all his former soldiers. It was a bronze medal with a crowned 'A' and the date '*JULI U: AUGUST/1866*' on the obverse and '*NASSAU'S/KRIEGERN*' on the reverse. The ribbon was orange with a thin blue edge. Over 5,200 medals were issued, with the King of Prussia again sanctioning its continued use.

The Saxon medal for 1866 was a bronze *cross pattée* with a small starburst in each arm with a central orb, edged with laurel and oakleaves, containing a crown and underneath the cypher of King Johann on the obverse and the numbers '*1866*' on the reverse. It was on a yellow ribbon with three light blue stripes. Saxony also awarded a campaign medal for the action in Schleswig-Holstein (then part of Denmark) in the winter of 1863–1864 consisting of a bronze *cross pattée* with central wreath enclosing the royal cypher under a crown on the obverse and the dates '*1863*' over '*1864*' on the reverse. The medal hung on a yellow ribbon with a light blue stripe close to each edge.

Bavaria issued a cross to all who took part in the 1866 campaign. It was a blackened bronze *cross pattée* with rounded ends to the cross, a heraldic Bavarian lion in the centre and the number '*1866*' on the reverse. The ribbon was white with two light blue stripes at each edge.

Baden's medal was of bronze, the decoration being instituted in 1839 by Grand Duke Leopold and was awarded as a general service medal and for specific campaigns. The face with a crowned griffin rampant, a sword in its right hand, a shield bearing the arms of Baden in its left, above a cannon and cannon balls on a plinth, inscribed above '*FÜR BADENS EHRE*' ('For Baden's Honour') and the reverse was inscribed '*LEOPOLD / FÜR / TREUEN DIENST / IM / KRIEGE*' ('Leopold for Loyal Service in War') within a circular wreath of oak leaves. The ribbon was yellow with a red stripe near each edge.

Prussia's allies also issued medals for the 1866 campaign. The battalion of the Principality of Lippe fought in the western German theatre with the Army of the Main and the award was a bronze medal with the initials of the prince under a royal crown on the obverse and '*1866*' within a laurel wreath on the reverse. The ribbon was red edged with thin white and yellow stripes. Less than 1,000 were issued.

The state of Waldeck-Pyrmont issued a cross for bravery to officers only. It was a silver Maltese cross with the face bearing a circular central red enamel medallion with the silver crowned cipher of Prince Georg Viktor zu Waldeck und Pyrmont within a silver-gilt border, and the reverse showing a circular central silver medallion inscribed '*FÜR / VERDIENST*' ('For Merit'). The ribbon was white with thin lines of yellow, red and black close to the edges.

Food

It was an almost impossible task for troops to be supplied daily by the commissariat when on the march. Therefore, some thought had been given to what and how much each man could carry with him. Potatoes, though a favourite with German troops, were too bulky and heavy to be carried and rice was used as a substitute. (However, in the right season potatoes were the main object of foraging parties, official or otherwise.) Bacon, sausage (the smoked continental variety), biscuits, coffee and salt formed the basis of all soldier's rations. Fresh meat could not be carried as it spoilt too quickly, as did bread. Meat 'on the hoof' was one answer, but not always practicable. A Prussian Army corps, drawn up and ready to march would, ideally, have eight days rations in their packs, bread-bags and pockets. The supply column would follow the line of march to replenish each day's used rations. Both French and German armies used the system of requisitions on the local inhabitants of the districts they passed through, supposedly paying for what they took, sometimes with coin, other times with paper promises and sometimes with neither. Other commodities, such as wood to make fires to cook whatever food they had, came from fields, farms and fences – anything that would burn. The countryside was also swept clean of hay and straw for bedding. Any houses in towns or villages or isolated farms were taken over to shelter troops at night, although the French did have their tents and poles strapped to their packs. Most troops were expected to find refreshment where they could, be it a local inn or *chateau*. Water courses quickly became polluted, which led to illness and disease, and the water-bottles carried by the French troops were highly prized, even by the Germans, for their capacity and robustness. However, it was not unusual to keep even the smaller Prussian glass bottles filled with something more stimulating than plain water. Part of every German regiment was the civilian sutler who sold little extras to the troops, such as wine or schnapps, sausage or whatever else was worth selling (how they managed to keep themselves supplied is a mystery!). The French had their official regimental *cantinières* who fulfilled a similar function.

Iron rations

The industrialist Heinrich Grueneberg of Berlin developed the pea sausage (*Erbswurst*) in 1867, and the patent was purchased for the equivalent of £6,000 by the Prussian government after rigorous testing

A Prussian sutler's wagon, with unit marked on the canvas tilt. (*Illustrirte Zeitung*)

showed that soldiers could thrive on it and bread alone. Pea sausage was a sort of dried pea soup with pork fat that did not spoil. After preparation at the factory, it was dried and formed into a sausage shape and wrapped in paper before being issued to the troops. To use in the field, a piece was cut from the sausage and dropped into a pan of boiling water, producing a nourishing and tasty soup, so the official line goes. The Knorr Company later purchased the product and manufactured the pea sausage for the German Army until 1918, although a similar dried pea soup was issued until 1945. Commercial production for the civilian market only ceased in 2018. At the outbreak of the war in 1870, a factory was built in Berlin at government expense, in which 1,700 workers eventually produced as much as 5,000 tons of pea soup sausage at a rate of 65 tons per day.

Both sides also resorted to the baked biscuit as part of the iron rations. However, these foods were only allowed to be eaten on the orders of an officer if the regular supply could not reach the men in the field. The French were supplied with bags of rice, pieces of bacon and loaves of bread, but a comment was made during the campaign that you could follow a French army by the piles of food dumped along the line of march. The French bread was not the baguette we know today, but the large round 'country' loaf seen on the shelves of modern baker's shops. And it could be several days old before it got to its intended destination. A French officer noted in his diary seeing a field beside a road (obviously used by a field bakery or a supply column dump) full of mouldering loaves as the commissariat had no means of distributing them.

Medical Services

The huge numbers of wounded after Sadowa had swamped the Prussian medical services. Disease and infection had spread rapidly in overcrowded field hospitals. In 1867 the best civilian and military doctors were called to Berlin, and their recommendations for reform were implemented over the next two years. The medical service was put in charge of a Surgeon General and army doctors were given enhanced authority and rank. Sanitary arrangements for the health of troops in the field were revised and their enforcement became part of the regular duties of troop commanders, who were also issued with pamphlets explaining their responsibilities under the 1864 Geneva Convention. Troops were issued with individual field dressings to staunch bleeding. Medical units were created, and all their personnel issued with Red Cross armbands. The units included stretcher-bearers trained in first aid who would be responsible for evacuating the wounded from the front to field hospitals. From there evacuation to base hospitals would be by rail using specially fitted-out hospital trains. The concept of medical personnel as non-combatants was not yet established and stretcher bearers were armed with carbines or pistols and doctors carried swords, but perhaps more as a mark of rank as they were rated as officers. Once back in Germany, where the new Red Cross movement was taken very seriously, the wounded would be cared for with the help of civilian doctors assisted by volunteer nurses recruited and trained under the active patronage of Queen Augusta of Prussia. Yet there was no conflict of authorities in wartime, nor any room for civilian volunteers wandering about the combat zone under their own devices. The work of civilian doctors and nurses was directed by a central military authority in Berlin. Like the artillery, the medical service was transformed between 1866 and 1870 by a systematic approach to overcoming the problems experienced in modern war. Organisation was one thing, why the system broke down was the sheer numbers of wounded left on the field after every engagement large or small. At the Battle of Gravelotte, the Germans lost over 20,000 men killed or wounded, the French nearly 16,000. It was little wonder that some men were left for days before being found and taken to dressing stations already swamped with casualties.

German field hospital treating wounded in the open.

Moving the wounded to railway wagons. (*Illustrirte Zeitung*)

The enemy providing a burial with military honours for a senior French officer.

Volunteers flocked to France soon after the outbreak of the war to help with the wounded of both sides. Many of these volunteers came as 'ambulances', more of a mobile hospital than just a mode of conveyance from the battlefield. There was a suspicion that the Irish ambulance when it arrived in France was overburdened with drivers and helpers, who had used the medical organisation to get to the seat of the war and many disappeared to join the Foreign Legion!

Uniforms

In the nineteenth century the manufacture of uniforms was undertaken by the state through government factories and private contractors. As cost was of paramount importance the quality of the finished article varied from adequate to barely passable to downright shoddy. Patterns and standards of finish were usually part of a contract between army departments and private suppliers, but quality control was not always practiced. Shoes were always a problem in any army, either they fell apart after a couple of weeks of use or the hobnails driven into the soles came through the material with terrible consequences to the feet of the wearer! The quality of greatcoats supplied to British soldiers in the Crimea became a national disgrace after it was revealed in the newspapers by correspondents accompanying the army in the field.

Soldier's memoires constantly refer to the quality of, or the lack of, coats, headwear and particularly, boots and shoes. Every soldier carried in his pack the equivalent of the British Army's 'Housewife' – a collection of needles, thread, buttons, cloth patches and everything useful to keeping a soldier's uniform in decent condition. Nevertheless, after a month in the field, the once pristine parade dress started to look shabby and new pieces of equipment, scarves, sashes, coats, bags and water-bottles made their appearance. Company tailors did what they could to alleviate the situation and the German armies particularly made use of captured stocks where practicable. This has not been well recorded, but official proclamations make it clear that it was being done. One German general banned the wearing of French National Guard trousers when his battalion's legwear deteriorated as the broad red stripe on dark grey material was only worn by Prussian senior officers, hence the mention of a Prussian 'company of generals'! More importantly the use of French red trousers by German troops was banned as it led to identification problems when viewed from a distance. Later it was noted that during the harsh winter of 1870–1871 a German company had liberated some rolls of green felt from a billiard table factory and turned it into warm mittens.

Officers of both sides fared better as generally they had their uniforms made privately by professional tailors, the quality of material and finishing being much superior to that of the common soldier. Footwear was of good serviceable material; where the soldier had his regulation boots and shoes, officers had fine leather items, made to measure and usually of a pattern that finished higher up the calf. Mention is made in the uniform descriptions of individual units of officer's use of gloves. These items were part of parade wear and therefore battle dress and were made of kidskin. In France and Prussia all officers and senior NCOs wore gloves, even if it is not mentioned in the body of the following uniform descriptions. Cavalry may have had more than one style: gauntlet cuffs for mounted duty and plain for foot duties.

It seems that every war occurs just when armies are in the process of changing their uniforms, with the French cavalry being a case in point. Hence some French hussars went on campaign in multicoloured uniforms, while others had the new blue tunics. Even within battalions there were differences: the Bavarian infantry was modifying its helmet and where the private soldiers continued with the old model, officers in the same company would have purchased a model of the new pattern.

The uniform descriptions generally follow the official regulations and photographs of existing items and no doubt many soldiers were issued and marched off to war in that dress. However, within days of the opening of the campaign, the picture would look completely different! The grenadiers of the Imperial Guard marched out of Paris in their full-dress bearskins, which were quickly substituted with field caps or kepis.

2

The Armed Forces of France

The basic infantry unit for command and administration in the French Army was the company, ideally of 120 men. Eight companies made up a battalion. Six companies took the field with the other two remaining in the depot to organise and train incoming reservists. A battalion therefore consisted of about 700 men. A *chasseur* battalion was similarly arranged. An infantry regiment, in the field, could consist of anything up to 2,100 men depending on battle casualties, sickness, detachments or missing reservists.

The squadron was the equivalent unit in the cavalry. The heavy cavalry was made up of ten regiments of cuirassiers, the line cavalry of 12 regiments of dragoons and eight regiments of lancers (all of which had five squadrons). The light cavalry, made up of hussars and the *chasseurs à cheval*, had six squadrons. Around 160 men formed the compliment of a squadron. As with the infantry, each regimental depot retained one squadron. A regiment of heavy or line cavalry could put 500 men into the field, and a light cavalry regiment around 600.

Organisation of the French Army

In 1868 the peacetime French line army was organised as follows:

100 regiments of infantry, 94 of 2,000 men and six of 2,300 (these last based in Africa)	201,800
3 regiments of zouaves of 3,600 men	10,800
19 battalions of *chasseurs* of 800 men and one of 900 (in Africa)	16,100
3 battalions of French Light Infantry (North Africa)	3,000
Foreign Legion (North Africa)	3,000
3 regiments of *tirailleurs* (*turcos*) (North Africa)	10,500
7 discipline companies	1,050
1 company of veteran NCOs	100
1 company of veteran fusiliers	200
Total infantry	246,550
30 regiments of cavalry of five squadrons	24,090
18 regiments of cavalry of six squadrons	17,244

4 regiments of *chasseurs d'Afrique*	4,496
2 regiments of *chasseurs* (in Africa)	2,036
3 regiments of *spahis*	3,489
Remount troops	2,967
Cavalry schools	242
Total cavalry	54,564
15 field artillery regiments of 1,500 men	23,430
1 bridging regiment	1,570
4 horse artillery regiments	4,580
10 companies of artillery labourers	1,540
6 companies of 'fire workers'	624
1 company of armourers	104
Total	34,064
3 regiments of engineers of 2,160 men	6,480
2 companies of workmen	224
Total	6,704
Transport train	8,304
Clerical	550
Medical	4,700
Administrative staff	5,611
Total	19,165
Gendarmerie, including the Guard Regiment	21,556
Total troops of the line	414,019

The cavalry, artillery, engineers and transport troops also included 75,545 horses, the *Gendarmerie* a further 13,897.

Weapons

In the early 1840s the French Army introduced its first percussion system rifles: the Model 1842 and the Model 1822T (meaning 'Transformation' of Model 1822 flintlock). Both weapons are recognisable by the shape of the plate holding the hammer, with the original for the 1822 model, and with the hammer moved forward for the 1842 model.

In 1854, the regiments of grenadiers and *Voltigeurs de la Garde* were equipped with the first rifled model, the Model 1854. The model for the grenadiers was a little longer than that of the *voltigeurs*. The weapon also equipped the *Génie* and the *Gendarmerie de la Guard*. The French line infantry adopted the rifled barrel a few months before the Italian War of 1859. The infantry rifles adopting this improvement were the Model 1842T (by transformation of the old Model 1842, the original barrel being rebored) and the Model 1857 (by refurbishing the Model 1842 guns with a new lock). Some of the Model 1822Ts were also transformed by rifling of the original gun barrel (and thus becoming Model '1822T bis' rifles). The loading was carried out from the muzzle, and detonation was by a percussion cap struck by a hammer.

After 1866 and the Prussian victory at Königgrätz, which was seen as a national disgrace for France, the Imperial Army adopted several new ideas which modernised and improved the effectiveness of its soldiers. Drill regulations emphasised the use of the close order in the attack and field practice made it seem a battle-winning tactic. It certainly had been against the Austrians in 1860. For many years French doctrine had been 'attack' at all costs and keep moving forward using the terrain to advantage. Indeed, during the Crimean War it had been noted that a French battalion moving forward built up its own momentum, even when the commander lost his nerve and ordered 'Halt', every other member of the battalion, from company officers to the lowest private continued to advance with everyone shouting *En avant, en avant!* ('Forward, forward!').

Furthermore, with the encouragement of the emperor himself, the rifle perfected over many years by Alphonse Chassepot (the Model 1866) was ordered into full production and immediately began to be issued to the troops. It fired a cartridge with ball, powder and primer all wrapped in a paper case, which was consumed on firing. As early as November 1867 a French regiment sent to defend the Pope and armed with the new rifle stopped Garibaldi in his tracks at Mentana on the road to Rome. Tests made with the Model 1866 showed it to be an effective weapon, with a range of 1,200 metres. It could fire six or seven 11mm rounds per minute, and the ammunition was light enough to allow every soldier to carry 90 rounds. Factories in France and selected foreign manufacturers got to work and by July 1870 more than a million weapons had been produced. Cavalry regiments were equipped with a shorter, carbine version. In most circumstances this would have been a war winner, and it gave the French soldier enormous confidence in his equipment.

French arsenals had been left with a vast number of excellent muzzle-loading rifles and were given the task of converting these to breech-loading. The result was what looked like a snuff box fitted to the breech which gave these weapons their nickname, '*à la tabatière*'. Over 350,000 had been converted by the beginning of the war. They were fired through the action of a hammer striking a pin to ignite the cartridge. They were less efficient than the Chassepot and with a slower rate of fire, so initially only issued to second-line troops (*Gardes Mobiles* and *Gardes Nationale*). This still left the French with nearly 1.5 million muzzle-loaders in store. The Chassepot was fitted with a sword bayonet with a slightly curved blade referred to as a '*yataghan*', based on a Turkish-style sword or dagger, originally introduced into the French Army in 1840. The converted *tabatière* rifles were issued with their original spike bayonet.

Napoleon III had been pursuing another war-winning idea, which was kept literally under wraps until war was declared. It resembled an artillery piece with large barrel and wooden carriage but was in fact a mechanical rapid fire volley gun (rather than a true machine gun) with 25 rifle barrels grouped together which were loaded with a pre-charged block and fired by rotating a handle producing a rate of fire of 100 rounds a minute. The '*Mitrailleuse*' also produced a terrible noise which could be quite demoralising to troops having to face it. By 1870, 215 of these fearsome weapons lay in the artillery depots ready for use. While the Chassepot rifle demanded changes in drill as to its use, the *Mitrailleuse* was a superb defensive weapon as events would prove, although no battlefield tactics had yet been formalised. Its range was little more than the Chassepot and a lot less than a light artillery piece, so how was one to deploy it? In the end it served with the artillery batteries, which much reduced its effectiveness. Another feature of the weapon was that all the bullets fired with a single turn of the handle tended to strike the same spot. A comment made by the Germans disparaging the weapon was 'Why use 25 bullets to kill a soldier when one would do?'.

Contemporary illustration of a French 'volley gun', the mitrailleuse.

Up to 1870 the French artillery used the 'La Hitte' system, introduced in 1858, which was a muzzle-loader with a bronze rifled barrel. The La Hittes fired time-fused ammunition, which had half a dozen settings, but for ease of use in the field was restricted to just two: short range of about 1,400–1,800 metres; and long range of about 2,400 metres. Two models were in use: a so-called '4-pounder' of 86mm calibre that fired a shell weighing 3.7kg; and a '12-pounder' of 121mm calibre with a shell weighing 11.5kg.

The French were not insensible to developments elsewhere in Europe and were experimenting with new models. One of these, constructed under the direction of an artilleryman, Lieutenant-Colonel Reffye, was a bronze-barrelled breech-loader designated 'canon de 7' (that is, classified as a 7-pounder, but actually firing a shell weighing 6.9kg). It had a calibre of 89mm. A prototype was successfully tested in June 1870, but it was not put into production until the fall of the empire.

In May 1867, the artillery was reorganised. In the Guard there was one regiment (field) of six batteries, two regiments (horse) of six batteries, and one Train squadron of two companies; and in the line the 1st to 15th regiments each had eight field and four foot batteries, the 16th (the *Pontoniers*) had 14 companies, the 17th to 20th regiments each had eight batteries of horse artillery, and two regiments of artillery train with 12 companies at first, later increased to 16. Through this reorganisation, a total of 164 batteries were established, of which 38 were horse artillery. It was decided that the *Mitrailleuse* was to be entrusted to the artillery. The 164 batteries, each of six guns, were thus distributed: 38 horse artillery batteries with rifled 4-pounders (*pièce de quatre*), 72 field batteries with rifled 4-pounders, 24 *Mitrailleuse* batteries, and 30 reserve batteries with 12-pounders.

Heavy cavalry swords and light cavalry sabres were in the main slight improvements on First Empire models. The Model 1822 had a four-bar brass guard with a straight blade for cuirassiers and a slightly curved blade for dragoons and light cavalry. Infantry officers carried a sword with a simple brass guard. All swords were carried in a steel scabbard. The Guard had models of their own.

Manpower

The development of technology appeared to be in hand, but that left the great sinew of war – manpower. The term of service for French conscripts was seven years, at the age of 21 every man drew what was, in effect, a lottery ticket. Depending on the number drawn, a 'good number' meant the conscript was free to go without further military obligation and a 'bad number' meant being drafted into a first contingent but, depending on the military budget, might not have to serve the full term. A second contingent number meant a few weeks training before being sent home as a reserve. Whatever the number drawn, if a family had money, the conscript could buy themselves out. The system allowed for the money to be used to pay time-expired men to re-enlist. At any one time up to 15 per cent of the army's personnel were re-enlisted old soldiers.

French MPs continually limited the military budget and blocked new expenditure which kept the army permanently below strength. Napoleon III strove to increase its numbers to around 800,000 men and supported the idea of a territorial reserve, along the lines of the Prussian *Landwehr*. Minister of War Marshall Niel tried to carry out Napoleon's policy but was blocked by military conservatives, radicals, the middle classes and the peasantry, represented by members of the legislature who were fearful of losing their seats. When the new law came into force in February 1868, it was so watered down to be almost useless. The new *Garde Mobile* should have had to do 25 days service annually, but this was reduced to 15 days and the men could go home at the end of each day! When the *Garde Mobile* was called out it nearly caused riots. A serious blow was the death of Marshall Niel in 1869; the new Minister of War, Marshal Le Boeuf, did not carry on the policy with any vigour, starved of cash and fearful of arming a section of the population who were opposed to the empire. On paper the *Garde Mobile* was a respectable force, but only on paper. It lacked weapons, uniforms, training, organisation and men.

The infantry troops of the line were supposed to be organised into ten army corps (on paper at least) of 24 divisions, 49 brigades and 98 regiments in France; the remaining troops, based in North Africa, were not part of this corps organisation. The cavalry was formed into four divisions with 12 brigades. However, the corps organisation was only applied to the Imperial Guard, and the 2nd, which had been based at the special 'camp of instruction' at Chalons (a vast training ground set up on an open, windy plain each year for training and manoeuvring large numbers of troops). On the outbreak of the war, it was transported to St Avold, south of Sarrbruck. The 1st Corps was a new formation, with troops from garrisons in Alsace and regiments brought over from Algeria, the zouaves and the *Turcos*. The 3rd Corps was the garrison of Paris, rushed by rail to Metz. The 4th Corps was made up of units from all over France and sent to Thionville, north of Metz near to the frontier with Luxemburg. The 5th Corps was from the Army of Lyon and was forwarded to the area around Bitsche near the Prussian border. The 6th Corps was intended to be the army reserve and gathered at the camp at Chalons. The 7th Corps was drawn from garrisons in the south of France and posted to southern Alsace around Belfort and Colmar. The 8th Corps was intended to be part of the army reserve, but was never formed, while the 9th was allocated to troops assembled at Belfort, but the circumstances of the campaign swept past the fortress and so its role was abandoned. The 10th Corps was to be a reserve corps formed from troops in Paris, but again was not put into effect. These last three corps no longer appeared in French orders of battle. Further corps were planned, the 11th was to be made up from regimental depots and the 12th was formed in August 1870 with units from the 6th Corps. As the war progressed and new armies were organised further corps numbers were allocated to them, and several discrete corps were raised within the besieged city of Paris.

The garrison of Algeria comprised the staff (senior officers, interpreters, etc.), nine regiments of infantry including the Foreign Legion, three battalions of light infantry, three battalions of zouaves, three battalions of *tirailleurs*, seven discipline companies, three regiments of *spahis*, eight squadrons of *chasseurs d'Afrique*, remounted veteran troops, sappers, six batteries of artillery and transport troops, making a total of 54,321.

On a war footing the compliment of the army was increased to include regimental depots, the infantry of 1,022 men, the cavalry of 314 men, artillery, *Gendarmerie* and even 1,572 men of the *Sapeurs Pompiers* (the militarised fire brigades), for a total of 184,000 men. By 1870, the armed forces, including the army at full strength, reserves, recruits of the year 1869 and the Algerian Army, was increased to 662,000. In the infantry battalions the former elite companies, the grenadiers and *voltigeurs*, were disbanded and the men distributed among the companies as 'first class soldiers' – in effect, lance corporals.

Marshal MacMahon, leading from the front.

The Imperial Guard formed a separate corps of two divisions of infantry and one division of cavalry. The infantry retained the former 'elite' titles, the first division comprised four regiments styled *voltigeurs*, plus a battalion of *chasseurs à pied*, the second division with three regiments styled grenadiers and a regiment of zouaves. The Guard Artillery consisted of a regiment of field artillery of six batteries and a regiment of horse artillery also of six batteries and a squadron of Train troops, totalling over 32,500 men. (This figure and the others given for the following corps totals are 'paper' figures and in no way reflect the actual numbers of troops assembled.)

The 1st Corps had four divisions of infantry and one division of cavalry of three brigades under Marshall MacMahon, Duke of Magenta, with a total in excess of 55,000 men. The 2nd Corps, commanded by General Frossard, had three divisions of infantry and one of cavalry, making a total of 38,000 men. The 3rd Corps at Metz under Marshall Bazaine had four divisions of infantry and one division of cavalry, a total of in excess of 47,000 men. The 4th Corps, commanded by General Ladmirault, had three infantry divisions and one of cavalry, for a total of 38,000 men. The 5th Corps under Generally de Failly, with a similar formation as above, totalled 38,000 men. The 6th Corps, the reserve army, led by Marshall Canrobert, had four infantry divisions and one of cavalry, making a combined strength of over 40,000 men. The 7th Corps, commanded by General Felix Douai, had three divisions of infantry and one of cavalry, around 40,000 men. The newly formed 12th Corps, instituted in August as a result of the early battles, drew some units from the 6th Corps and consisted of three infantry divisions and two cavalry divisions, for a total of 33,000 men.

Uniforms

Every French regular soldier had items of uniform issued to him, or if an officer, had items made to specified patterns. Every soldier had a number of duties, from engaging an enemy in combat on the battlefield to sweeping out the barracks, and for each duty there was an order of dress. As an example, here is a quotation from regulations for the Artillery of the Guard issued in 1864:

Combat

1. *Grand tenue de service* (full best dress)
2. *Tenue de service* (service dress)
3. *Tenue de manœuvre* (undress service)
4. *Tenue de route et de campagne* (marching campaign dress)
Non-combat duties
5. *Grande tenue de service* (full dress)
6. *Tenue du jour de service* (daily wear)
7. *Tenue du jour ordinaire* (ordinary day wear)
8. *Tenue de matin* (morning dress, that is, formal walking out)
9. *Tenue de cérémonie* (officer's full ceremonial dress)
Added to this some Guard units had a 'court' and 'ball' order of dress and an evening dress.

Units of the Army

Cent-gardes

The most senior unit of the French Army was the squadron of '*Cent-gardes*', which was an elite unit reminiscent of the former aristocratic royal bodyguards. It was not part of the Imperial Guard. Created in March 1854 it consisted of 148 officers and men who acted as guards to the emperor wherever he was resident and a mounted escort when he travelled and provided a personal guard on campaign. Napoleon III took a personal interest in these troops and he and the squadron commander, Colonel Verly, made decisions as to uniforms and arms without reference to any other body. The squadron was armed with a unique breech-loading rifled-barrel weapon designed by Antoine Hector Thésée Treuille de Beaulieu, then a captain, but seconded to the Chatellerault arms factory. It was a carbine firing a 9mm pinfire cartridge and fitted with an enormous sword bayonet, a metre in length (*sabre-lance*). Treuille de Beaulieu was also instrumental in the design of the rifling of the La Hitte artillery system and the Chassepot rifle (see above). He also designed a pistol version of his carbine, but it did not see service.

In common with all other branches of the French Army the *Cent-gardes* had various orders of dress, depending on the duties they were performing. However, as they had so many different duties they had a great number of uniforms, more than any other unit of the Imperial Army. Officer's dress, mounted, consisted of: steel helmet with silver plate and gilded chin scales, plate and comb, white tuft, known as a '*houpette*' on the top of the comb, a white horsehair mane falling from the comb and scarlet plume rising from a gold olive; polished steel breast and backplate under which was worn a quilted waistcoat edged with scarlet cloth and gold braid; a long sky-blue tunic with a red collar, cuffs and piping and lining to the skirts that were turned back when mounted, gold lace tab on each side of the collar with gold bridles to secure the gold epaulettes, blue cuff flaps, gold buttons, nine down the front, three on each false pocket at the back and three on each cuff flap; white riding breeches and black knee-high boots; white gloves with large gauntlet cuffs; gold aiguillette on left shoulder; and white pouch belt. The guard rode black horses with square-cut red shabraques with broad gold lace edging.

Full dress on foot was similar, but the tunic skirts were not turned back. For full dress on duty within a palace, the breast and backplate was replaced with a sleeveless cloth garment, the '*soubreveste*', bordered with gold and decorated with an imperial coat of arms also in gold. For walking out dress, the tunic with epaulettes and aiguillette was worn, but with red trousers with a double blue stripe down the outside seam.

The headgear was a small black bicorne hat with a tricolour cockade. White gloves without cuffs completed the outfit.

For morning dress, the bicorne was replaced by a kepi with a red top and gold band with a gold 'N' below a crown at the front, or the field cap, the '*bonnet de police*', sky-blue body with wide gold lace, red top, piped in gold with a gold tassel. (Just to make it confusing, the official name of the kepi was the '*bonnet de police* with peak', the *bonnet de police*, or field cap was shaped like a British side cap, but worn on the top of the head, similar to the Austrian field cap of the period. It was originally a type of stocking cap, but by 1870 this had become a coloured top, decorated with a contrasting colour piping and a tassel at the front.) Trousers were red, with a double gold stripe for officers and double blue stripe for NCOs and guards.

There were two types of gala dress for receptions at a palace: a sky-blue tailcoat with red facings and red trousers, or black breeches and white silk stockings. For balls, the blue tailcoat with white breeches and stockings and buckled shoes were worn. When the guardsmen accompanied the emperor while hunting, they wore a green tunic with red collar and cuffs edged with gold lace, a white panel with gold lace with eight or nine gold buttons down the centre of the tunic and the gold lace continuing down to the bottom of the skirts. Further items included white breeches, high black boots and white gloves. Headgear was a small black tricorn edged with gold lace. A white waistbelt supported a short dress sword in a black leather scabbard. Napoleon, himself, wore this costume while hunting and the empress had a version with gold lace *boutonnières* (flat lace buttonhole decoration).

The non-commissioned officers (NCOs) and guardsmen wore basically the same uniform, but with polished steel helmets and brass fittings. The epaulette fringes and aiguillette were mixed red and gold. Officers and NCOs carried a straight-bladed sword in full dress and guardsmen the *sabre-lance*. For walking out dress, the *Cent-gardes* wore a small epee-type sword carried in a black leather scabbard.

Guardsmen had a short tunic for exercises that was sky-blue with red collar and cuff flaps piped yellow, red shoulder straps piped yellow and yellow piping round the pocket flaps and down the front and round the skirts of the tunic. They wore red trousers with double blue stripes, high riding boots, the *bonnet de police*, and white gloves without cuffs. They also had a stable dress of a short waistcoat in sky-blue closed with nine yellow metal buttons. It had a blue collar, cuffs and shoulder straps, with a small red tab on the front of the collar and two further buttons on the sleeve, one on and one above the cuff as well as two small pockets on the waist. White trousers, shoes and the *bonnet de police* were also worn. For bad weather Guardsmen were issued a long riding coat in sky-blue with a cape that extended to the elbows and a red collar with yellow buttonhole lace bars.

Trumpeters had a red tunic, lined with sky-blue. Each button was decorated with gold 'Brandenburg' lace and the sleeves had gold inverted chevrons from cuff to shoulder. They carried a long straight silver trumpet, designed by Adolphe Sax, better known for his saxophone. The trumpet was adorned with a square banner in red and sky-blue with the Imperial arms in the centre. The trumpeters rode grey horses.

There was a plan to appoint a *cantinière* for the squadron, but it was never followed through. A uniform was designed and made, but it was only worn once, by the wife of Colonel Verly and then at a ball at the Tuileries Palace.

The Imperial Guard

The 1st division (*voltigeurs*) of the Imperial Guard infantry consisted of two brigades with two regiments of three battalions plus a battalion of *chasseurs*. The divisional troops included two batteries of 4-pounders and one of *Mitrailleuse* from the Guard foot artillery regiment and an engineer company. The 2nd division (grenadiers) consisted of two brigades: the first having a regiment of grenadiers with three battalions and a regiment of zouaves with two battalions; and the second having two regiments of grenadiers. The divisional troops were the same as those of the 1st division. Each infantry battalion had seven companies, six of which served in the field, except for the *chasseur* battalion which had ten, of which eight served in the field.

Two regiments of the *voltigeurs* were created in 1854 and two others in 1857 following the Crimean campaign. The *voltigeurs* played only a minor role in the War of 1870. Their uniform consisted of a black leather shako, shaped higher at the back (18cm) and with just enough space at the front (13cm) for a brass eagle plate (12.2cm high), the eagle standing on a globe with bolts of lightning. The number of the regiment was shown as a cut out on the globe. A painted metal tricolour cockade was situated behind the eagle's head with a red and yellow plume in full dress. In undress, the plume was replaced by a yellow pompon. The shako had a leather 'V' shaped strips at the side with a black painted metal ventilation hole between the arms of the 'V' and a black leather chin strap. The shako was quickly discarded in the field and replaced by a *bonnet de police*, shaped like a side cap with a blue body edged with yellow lace and a red top, decorated with a yellow grenade and piping and a tassel which hung down at the front. Officers had a kepi with a red top broad yellow lower band decorated with gold piping and lace and a small gold grenade badge on the front.

The *voltigeur*'s tunic was dark blue and single-breasted. It was closed by nine brass buttons, each buttonhole decorated with strips of pointed lace covering the chest of the tunic (*boutonnières*). The buttons were stamped with a crowned imperial eagle and the letters 'GARDE IMPERIALE'. The tunic had a yellow collar with a small blue grenade on either side, blue pointed cuffs piped yellow and with two small buttons on the rear, a button on each shoulder to fix the epaulettes and two buttons on each of the false pocket flaps at the rear skirts as well as a further button to the small strip of cloth to hold the waistbelt in position. The pocket flaps, rear skirts and retaining strap were all piped yellow, as was the front of the tunic. The bridles to hold the epaulettes were yellow and the epaulettes themselves were red with yellow half-moons. Red trousers, with a broad blue stripe down the outside seem, were tucked into white gaiters above black shoes. The waistbelt was white, although the shoulder straps and pack straps were black leather. The belt had a large brass buckle embossed with a grenade and hunting horn. A small black leather expense pouch hung at the right front of the belt, a larger pouch at the rear with an eagle and hunting horns on the flap and the Chassepot bayonet in a steel scabbard. Each man had a white bread-bag, the strap over the right shoulder and a metal water bottle in a blue cloth covering suspended from a black belt over the left shoulder. The brown cowhide pack on the back had the tent section strapped round it and the poles and pegs. The steel mess tin was strapped to the pack. In bad weather the troops had a blue knee-length cloak with a large turn-down collar, closed by four brass buttons decorated with yellow *boutonnières*.

Officers wore a similar tunic to the men, but without the buttonhole lace. It had gilt buttons and grenades on the collar, gold epaulettes, and a black waistbelt supporting the epee-type sword in a black leather scabbard with a gilt knuckle bow with a black silk sword knot. The belt had a gilt snake-type fastening. All officers were entitled to wear a gold aiguillette from the right shoulder, although this was often dispensed with in the field. White gloves were worn in full dress. Full parade dress included the shako, tunic with gold *boutonnières*, gold waistbelt with two bands of yellow lace, and gilt gorget with silver eagle. Alternative full dress was similar, but with the bicorne in place of the shako, a black leather waistbelt, and no gorget. In field dress many officers wore the rolled greatcoat over the right shoulder and provided themselves with a coloured cummerbund (blue or red were popular shades), either over the tunic, or under it with several buttons undone to reveal it. Because of the amount of marching, often over broken terrain, some officers bought boots of various descriptions; high riding-type boots were popular in black or brown leather. It was not unusual to see officers carrying a water-bottle (not always for water!), field glasses in a leather case and privately purchased pistols of many different manufactures.

During the war of 1870, the *grenadiers* participated with the Army of the Rhine in the Battle of Rezonville where they were posted on the left flank. The total losses to the three regiments amounted to 1,200 men.

The third battalion of the third regiment did not take part in the battle as it was on escort duty with the emperor marching to Sedan. The rest were taken after the capitulation of Metz.

In imitation of his uncle, Napoleon dressed his grenadiers in a tall bearskin with a brass plate with an embossed eagle standing on lightning bolts and a large bomb on which the regimental number was shown as a cut out and a rear patch with a white grenade on a red ground. A small tricolour cockade on the left side from which a red plume was added in full dress. Although the grenadiers marched to the battlefield wearing the fur bonnet, it was quickly returned to the depot and replaced in the field by the *bonnet de police*, which had a blue body edged with red lace, blue top piped red with a red grenade badge at the front and a red tassel. Officers had a kepi with a red top piped gold, a blue base with a gold lace band and a gold grenade badge on the front as well as a false chin strap and black peak.

The grenadier's tunic was a similar style to the *voltigeurs* with the following differences: red collar, piped blue with a small white cloth grenade badge on each side; red piping down the front and on the rear pocket flaps; round red cuffs with a white three-pointed cuff flap with three small buttons; red epaulettes and epaulette bridles; and white *boutonnières*. The belt buckle was stamped with a large grenade. The ammunition pouch was decorated with an eagle plate and four grenades, one in each corner. The cloak had white *boutonnières*.

Officers had a similar uniform, although the brass bearskin plate, buttons and grenade collar badge were gilded, and the epaulettes and aiguillettes were gold. Parade dress was tunic with gold *boutonnières*, gold waistbelt and gorget, and bearskin with red plume. In undress, officers wore the tunic without buttonhole lace, the kepi and white gloves. This order of dress was worn in the field with the addition of a rolled greatcoat for officers styled a '*caban*' ('pea coat'), dark blue and closed with four black loops and toggles.

The *chasseurs à pied* battalion was created in 1854. It took part in the Crimean and Italian campaigns where it was awarded the *Legion d'honneur* for the capture of an Austrian flag. The battalion was severely engaged during the Battle of Rezonville where it lost 200 men. *Chasseurs à pied* wore the uniform introduced in 1854 consisting of a short dark blue tunic with blue collar and pointed cuffs piped yellow, yellow grenade badge on each side of the collar, yellow piping down the front of the tunic and on the false pocket flaps on the rear skirts which also had a yellow grenade badge. There were nine white metal buttons down the front of the tunic, two on each cuff, two at the rear on the false pockets, one on a loop of material on the left side to support the waistbelt and one on each shoulder to attach the epaulettes. Each button closing the tunic had a yellow braid ending in a Hungarian knot. The trousers were blue grey (95 per cent dark blue, 5 per cent white wool), cut very wide and finished halfway between knee and ankle. The side pockets were decorated with yellow piping. Below the trousers, *chasseurs* wore sheepskin leggings, yellow or brown, fitted at the side with black leather with buckles and laces. White gaiters were worn over the black shoes. Headgear was a black leather shako with a brass eagle plate, but it was quickly exchanged for a *bonnet de police*, blue with yellow lace and a blue top with yellow piping and tassel and a yellow bugle horn badge. A kepi was also available, with a blue top piped yellow, black body with yellow lace with a small yellow hunting horn badge. Epaulettes were green with yellow half-moons. Black leather belts and straps sported an ammunition pouch with eagle plate and a belt buckle with embossed grenade. *Chasseurs* had a short cape with a hood that was blue-grey and closed by four cloth covered buttons.

Officers had a long tunic, with very full skirts that fell in folds. It was dark blue with yellow piping round the collar and the pointed cuffs, and silver grenades on the collar. The trousers were blue grey with a double silver stripe down the outside seams. The black belt had a snake buckle, and a straight sword was carried in a steel scabbard with a black silk sword knot. The full parade dress tunic had silver braid decorating the buttons ending in Hungarian knots, silver epaulettes and a silver aiguillette from the right shoulder. The officer's kepi had a dark blue top with silver piping, a black lower band with silver lace and a silver hunting horn badge on the front. For service in the field officers adopted high boots, rolled greatcoat across the right shoulder, coloured cummerbunds and pistols of various types in brown or black holsters.

The *zouave* regiment was created in 1854 and was engaged during the Battle of Rezonville where it lost 95 men out of 1,200. The Zouaves of the Guard had its beginnings in companies raised in the French-occupied North Africa; by 1870 all personnel were European but they kept the original style of uniform. The zouave uniform was based on a short open jacket (the *shama*) which was dark blue with yellow lace at the edges and on the chest round the false pockets, with red pointed cuffs. Underneath it was a waistcoat that was buttoned on the right side with three tabs. The waistcoat was also blue with yellow lace around the neck and down the front and a plain cloth back. A blue cummerbund was worn over the waistcoat, but under the jacket. The baggy, Turkish trousers were similar to the *chasseurs*, but in red with yellow piping around the side pockets and down the outside. Leggings, gaiters and shoes were the same as those worn by the *chasseurs*. The headgear was a red cap, like a large fez (*chechia*), with a yellow cord and tassel at the top. Around the cap was a large white turban, which was left off in undress. The zouaves also wore a short, hooded cape, coloured mid-blue with four buttons decorated with red *boutonnières*. As the zouaves originally had been recruited in North Africa where it customary to grow a beard, the NCOs and men all grew their beard long.

The zouave officers did not follow the Arab dress of the men but wore a similar style of uniform to the *Chasseurs*, consisting of a dark blue tunic with gold grenades on the blue collar, red pointed cuffs, and gold epaulettes in full dress with gold epaulette bridles. The tunic was often worn open to reveal a light blue cummerbund and a black sword belt. Trousers were red with a broad blue stripe and black shoes were worn. Officers carried a sword with a three-bar brass hilt in a steel scabbard adorned with a black sword knot with a gold tassel. The officer's kepi had a red crown piped yellow, a blue base with a broad yellow lace and a small gilt grenade on the lace. A gilt false chin strap was displayed above the peak and the chin strap was made of black leather. As with all guard's officers, they were entitled to a gold aiguillette on the right shoulder.

The Guard *mounted artillery regiment* was formed in 1854. It was reformed in 1870 with two regiments of six batteries of six 4-pounders. The Guard *foot artillery* had a dark blue hussar-type dolman with a blue collar, laced with red and red pointed cuffs. It had 18 rows of red braid with a row of yellow metal buttons down the front and a further row of buttons at each end of the braid. The back of the dolman had red lace on the seams and five small buttons. This item was used for full dress, while on campaign they wore a simple blue waistcoat with a row of nine yellow metal buttons, a further button on each shoulder to secure the shoulder straps and a button on each cuff. The blue collar had a small three-pointed red tab. Trousers were dark blue with red piping on the seam and a red stripe either side of the seam. White gaiters were worn above black shoes.

The gunners wore a black fur busby decorated with a large red pompon and yellow metal chin scales. It was worn in the field as well as a kepi with a red crown piped blue, with a blue base. For camp dress a *bonnet de police* was issued, which had a dark blue base with broad red lace, blue top piped in red with a red tassel and grenade badge. Equipment consisted of a white shoulder belt attached to which was a small black leather cartridge pouch with an eagle and crossed cannon barrels in yellow metal on the flap. A white waistbelt was worn under the waistcoat supporting a sword bayonet in a steel scabbard. The gunners were originally armed with a Model 1829 carbine, but by 1870 had re-equipped with Chassepots. Their pack was of black leather carried on white shoulder straps. Round it, on three sides, was the double-breasted greatcoat, dark blue with two rows of four buttons and decorated with red *boutonnières*. In the field the artillery men also had a white cloth bread-bag and water-bottle.

In full dress the officer's dolman was officially dark blue, so dark that it had better be described as black with gold braid, and a gold pouch-belt and pompon on the front of the busby. Trousers with a black pouch belt replaced the red stripe with gold lace. Rank was shown by inverted gold chevrons above the cuffs. In campaign dress the braid was black and the buttons remained gold. The *bonnet de police* was of blue material with broad gold lace and a grenade badge on the base, gold piping and tassel. The kepi also dark blue with a gold band round the lower part and gold piping on the crown.

The sapper companies of the Guard *engineers* wore a tunic similar to those of the *voltigeurs* and grenadiers with yellow metal buttons and red *boutonnières*, a black collar with red grenade badge, blue round cuffs, piped red, black three-pointed cuff flaps also piped red, and red epaulettes, although sergeants and sergeant-majors had yellow half-moons. Trousers were as the artillery. There was a white waistbelt with black pack straps. The sappers wore a large black fur bearskin without a front plate, but with a small red tassel at the top (all that was left from the cords and flounders when the bearskin was introduced in 1854) and a red plume rising from a tricolour cockade on the left side. White gaiters were worn above black shoes. The sappers retained the black iron helmet and back and breast plate with brass studs, of the design introduced in 1838 for service in the trenches. It was worn over the plain waistcoat. The engineer's equipment drivers wore a hussar busby with a red pompon at the front with, in full dress, a red plume. A red bag hung down the left side. Drivers had riding trousers with leather false boots and were armed with a cavalry sabre with a white sword knot. The caped mantel was blue grey with four red *boutonnières*.

The *Train* was the transport service of the Army, and the Guard had its own Train squadron made up of six companies. In full dress it wore a mid-blue dolman with dark blue collar and cuffs both bearing wide red lace. While the dolman had red lace and piping on the back, the front was decorated with nine rows of red lace with narrow twisted cords between each. The dolman had a row of white metal buttons down the front and two further rows on each side. In full dress knotted red cords were worn across the chest from the right shoulder to the left, finishing with red flounders and tassels. There were red trousers with a double blue stripe for foot troops and riding trousers with false boots for mounted men. A shako decorated with red lace around the top and at the sides was worn in an oilskin cover in the field. For parade dress the shako had a red pompon with a red-over-black feather plume. Officers had silver fittings on their shako and silver stripes on their trousers, and the red dolman cords replaced with silver. The black pouch was worn on a silver belt. For undress there was a dolman with all black cords and black collar and cuffs, with a black leather pouch belt. Mounted men were armed with a cavalry sabre and a carbine. The kepi had a blue top with white piping and a black lower band, while officers had silver piping with a strip of silver lace on the lower band.

The Cavalry Division of the Imperial Guard

The cavalry division was made up of three brigades each of two regiments: light brigade (guides and *chasseurs à cheval*); medium brigade (dragoons and lancers); and heavy brigade (cuirassiers and carbineers). The division included two batteries of the Guard horse artillery regiment. The Guard cavalry regiments had six squadrons, five of which served in the field.

Originally there were two regiments of *carbineers*, but only one from 1865. It was not engaged during the war of 1870. The uniform was a light blue tunic with scarlet collar, cuff flaps on the blue cuffs and scarlet piping down the front of the tunic, round the cuff and on the rear skirts. There was a scarlet aiguilette on the right shoulder. The tunic had nine white metal buttons down the front and three on each false pocket flap at the rear and three on each cuff flap. A button on each shoulder was for the epaulettes and there was a further button to secure the small cloth tab at the left side of the tunic to support the waistbelt. The bridles on the point of each shoulder to hold the epaulettes were also scarlet. The skirts were lined with scarlet cloth and were buttoned back for full dress. Parade dress riding trousers were white with narrow legs and four small buttons at the ankles so they could fit into the knee-high black leather boots. Plain white canvas trousers were worn for stable dress and camp wear. In field dress, scarlet trousers with a light blue stripe were worn. The brass crested helmet had steel front plate and a red woollen crest on the comb. The cuirass was also brass with steel edging and a sunburst plate at the front. There was a black belt to hold the front and back plates together. Under the cuirass a buff-coloured padded vest edged red was worn. The special riding gloves had a yellow sheepskin hands and white gauntlet cuffs. Off duty and stable dress was a light blue waist-length jacket with nine white metal buttons, light blue collar and cuffs with small red tabs on the front of the collar. The *bonnet de police* was light blue with a wide white lace and tassel and grenade badge piped red. Arms were a long straight sword with a three-bar brass hilt carried in a steel scabbard. The sword knot was white with a red fringe. Horse furniture was light blue with white lace edging piped red. The saddle cloth had a white crown in the front corners and a white crown and 'N' in the rear corners. The rolled portmanteau had similar colours, also with a white crown on the ends. Officers had the same uniform, but with silvered and gilded metal parts, silver aiguilette and trouser stripe as well as a red greatcoat with a waist-length cape closed by four silver buttons.

The *cuirassier* regiment was created in 1854. It formed, along with the carabineers, the heavy brigade of the Guard. At Rezonville, it was ordered to hold the advance of the Prussian infantry. As a result, it suffered 250 casualties. The tunic of the cuirassiers was dark blue with white epaulettes and a white aiguilette on the right chest. Facings and buttons were the same as those worn by the carabineers. The helmet was steel with a brass plate chin scales and comb from which descended a black horsehair mane, with a red tuft on the front of the comb. In parade dress a red feather plume was worn from a brass holder on the left side of the helmet. Below the plume was a squadron colour pompon; all cavalry regiments followed the same system: 1st Squadron, dark blue; 2nd, crimson; 3rd, green; 4th, sky-blue; 5th, yellow; and white for regimental staff. A steel cuirass with brass shoulder scales and studs was worn on the chest. The *bonnet de police* was dark blue with decoration as the carabineers. A white pouch belt and black pouch completed the uniform.

The *Dragoon* regiment was created in 1855 and took the name of 'Empress's Dragoons' in 1857. Together with the lancers, it formed the medium brigade of the Guard. The regiment took part in the great cavalry action of Mars-la-Tour where it lost 70 men. The dragoons retained the old green coatee with a red collar and green-pointed cuffs piped red. There was red piping on the short coat tails with a red grenade badge on each turn-back. The coatee was single-breasted and closed by seven plain buttons. For full dress a white plastron was buttoned to the front of the coatee, the buttons brass with one button just below the shoulder and six on each side on the chest. In service dress the white plastron was replaced by a green one with red piping. White epaulettes and a white aiguilette were worn as well as a white waistbelt and pouch belt with a black pouch. The helmet was similar to that of the cuirassiers but made entirely of brass with a black tuft and mane, or a red plume for parade dress. The caped greatcoat was pale grey with four brass buttons with red *boutonnières* across the chest. Trousers were red with a double green stripe down the outside edge, separated by thin green piping. For mounted duties the trousers finished with leather false boot shafts over short spurred boots, whereas for foot duties the trousers were without the false boots. A white waistbelt with a brass buckle stamped with a grenade badge and white pouch belt were also worn. A sabre with a brass three-bar guard was held in a steel scabbard. For stable dress, there were plain white trousers, a waist-length single breasted jacket with nine buttons and a red tab on the front of the collar. The *bonnet de police* had a green body with red lace, piping and tassel. Officers had a gilded metal helmet and gilt epaulettes and aiguilettes as well as trousers with gold stripes in place of the green. They also had a green single-breasted waist-length jacket for undress, black waistbelt and a green *bonnet de police* with gold decoration, or a red kepi with a gold lower band and a small gold grenade badge and piping on the upper part. The greatcoat was green, double-breasted with the buttons arranged to resemble the plastron. In ceremonial dress a single-breasted tailcoat was worn with white knee breeches and stockings and black buckled court shoes.

With this dress the headgear was the felt bicorne and the sword was replaced by a short epee in a black leather scabbard tipped with gilt metal.

The *lancer* regiment was created in 1855. It took part in the great cavalry action of Mars-la-Tour where it lost 140 men. The full dress of the Lancers was a white single-breasted coatee, similar to the dragoons, closed by nine small bone buttons. It had a sky-blue collar, pointed cuffs and piping along the rear seams of the arms and back as well as sky-blue turn-backs on the small coat tails, red epaulettes and aiguilette. The brass buttons were arranged as those of the dragoons on a plastron that was sky-blue for parade dress and white for undress. In the field all ranks wore the sky-blue waist-length single-breasted stable jacket, with brass buttons and a white tab on the front of the collar, and red riding trousers with a double blue stripe for mounted duties and red trousers without the false boots for duties on foot. The shapka helmet had a black leather bowl and a peak with a brass edge, a sky-blue square top edged with white piping and a white band of lace between the bowl and the top. A large brass plate of a sunburst with a crowned 'N' in the centre was fitted to the front of the bowl. On the left side of the neck of the square top was a large tricolour cockade and a company-coloured pompon served as the base for the parade red feather plume. Fitted to the top right-hand corner of the square was a black chin strap covered by a brass chain, the other end attached to the left side chin scale boss in the shape of a lion's head. Red cap lines attached to the rear corner of the top tied round the neck and looped round the chest and under the left epaulette ending in flounders and tassels. The shapka was worn in a tight, fitted oilskin cover in most orders of dress. A second light shapka was issued which was made with a cardboard frame covered in a fitted oilskin for duties in the field. The *bonnet de police* was sky-blue with white lace and piping. The caped greatcoat was light grey with four white metal buttons and sky-blue *boutonnières*. Officers had the same dress, but with gold epaulettes and aiguilette and gilt buttons. Their shapka had a gilt band in place of the white and their stable jacket had white piping round the collar and cuffs and at the back of the sleeves and on the short turn-backs, but no collar tabs. Officer's trousers had gold stripes. The troopers white pouch belt was replaced by a gold belt with three blue stripes. The pouch belt had a red leather cover with gilt studs. The lancers were armed with a sabre, pistol and wooden lance which carried a white over red pennon that was removed in the field. Officers had a sky-blue greatcoat with the buttons arranged to resemble the plastron of the jacket. In the field officers had a kepi with a blue upper part, piped gold with a gold badge of crossed lances and a gold lace lower part.

Eight squadrons of *guides* were created in 1848 and they joined the light brigade of the Imperial Guard in 1855, but in 1870 they played only a minor role. A squadron formed the emperor's escort and was captured at Sedan. The guides had a hussar-style uniform, with a mid-green dolman and pelisse. The dolman had a green collar and red cuffs, both edged with yellow lace. The front was covered with 18 rows of yellow hussar lace with a central line of brass buttons and two further lines of buttons on each side. The back of the garment had more yellow lace and piping. The pelisse had six rows of hussar braiding and black fur edging and was hung around the body with a yellow cord. The guides did not have the usual Imperial Guard aiguilette, but a twisted cord across the chest ending in flounders and tassels on the left shoulder. Red riding trousers with double yellow stripes and leather false boots were worn along with a white pouch belt. Headgear was a large busby with a red bag, piped yellow and a tall white plume with a black base. These last two items were not worn in the field. The caped greatcoat was grey with four brass buttons and yellow *boutonnières*. Stable dress was a green waist-length jacket with a single row of buttons and red tabs on the corners of the collar. The *bonnet de police* was green with a red top and yellow piping. White belts and staps were worn. The full-dress sabretache was faced with green, edged in yellow lace, with an imperial coat of arms in the centre. In undress a second sabretache was issued in black leather but with the coat of arms. No sabretache was worn on campaign. The guides were armed with a sabre with a brass three-bar hilt and a carbine. The uniform worn by officers replaced the yellow braid with gold. The greatcoat was plain green double-breasted with two rows of seven buttons. There was also an officer's frock coat which extended to just above the knee that was green with a single row of 12 gilt buttons and piped in red round the collar, pointed cuffs and down the front. It was worn with red trousers. Officers had a different uniform for undress wear: the green dolman had the braid in black wool, with black lace round the top and bottom of the collar, round the cuffs and round the hem and the rear. The twisted cords and flounders were also black as was the leather pouch belt. The kepi had a red top and a green lower band with gold piping and cover to the chin strap. In the field or on manoeuvres a shako was worn, which had a cardboard structure covered with a tight-fitting oilskin and a gold rosette.

Four squadrons of *chasseurs à cheval* were created for service in the Crimea and a full regiment on their return. They played only a minor role during the campaign of 1870. The uniform was similar in style to the guides, sporting a green dolman with red cuffs. The lace and cords were white with white metal buttons. Red riding trousers with white stripes were worn. Stable dress was as for the guides, but with white buttons and the *bonnet de police* had white lace and tassel. The fur busby was slightly smaller than the guides model, but carried a longer red bag, piped white and a short white feather plume. Full dress sabretache was green with white borders and a central, brass Imperial arms; the undress one of black leather with the arms. The riding coat had silver buttons and green *boutonnières*. The officer's dress dolman had all cords, lace and piping in silver and a silver pouch belt as well as silver buttons and trouser stripes. In undress and campaign dress the dolman had all the silver replaced with black and the busby lost its bag and plume. The shako was as the guide's but with a silver rosette.

The Guard *horse artillery* regiment had six 4-pounder batteries. They wore a similar uniform to the foot artillery (see above), but with five rows of buttons on the red braid. The greatcoat was single-breasted with four yellow metal buttons and red *boutonnières*. For dismounted wear white trousers and a plain waistcoat with a single row of buttons was worn, whereas when mounted blue trousers with black false boots were worn. There was also a cavalry sword with a white sword knot and a blue sabretache edged with red lace and a crowned eagle and crossed cannon metal plate. The sabretache was not taken on campaign. The officers' dolman had gold braid and the blue trousers had a gold stripe in place of the red. Their sabretache was decorated with wide gold lace. The campaign dress dolman had black braid. In exercise dress officers had a plain blue greatcoat, double-breasted with two rows of gilt buttons. It was worn with plain blue trousers and high riding boots. In undress a dark blue pelisse was adopted, with six rows of black braid, black toggles and black fur trim. Headwear was the *bonnet de police*, dark blue with gold lace, piping, tassel and grenade badge. In ordinary working dress the officers had a plain dark blue tunic with nine gilt buttons, worn with the kepi. The officers of the Guard artillery did not wear the aiguillette.

Uniforms of the Line Infantry Regiments

Tunic

In 1867 the French infantry was authorised a new tunic (and a new shako), which was issued to the troops in 1868. The military authorities had been experimenting with tunics of different length, starting with a very long tunic, almost a frock coat, and later a single-breasted tunic that only extended slightly below the waistbelt. The new model was similar to English and Prussian designs, but it was double-breasted and closed by a row of seven brass buttons, the second row of buttons were 120mm apart at the neck and narrowed to 100mm apart at the waist. The tunic was further tailored at the waist. The basic colour was dark blue with a yellow collar, piped blue, yellow piping down the front of the tunic and around the 70mm wide blue cuffs. At the rear of the tunic there was yellow piping round two false pockets, each decorated with two buttons.

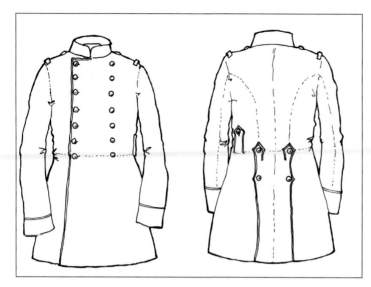

French infantry tunic, front and back views.

There were a further two small buttons on the shoulder next to the collar to secure the epaulettes and a small button holding a thin strip of blue-piped yellow material to hold the waistbelt in place. The tunic had a red grenade badge either side of the collar for grenadiers, replaced with a red hunting horn for the *voltigeurs*. There were red epaulettes for grenadiers, yellow for *voltigeurs* and green with red crescents for fusilier companies. Later in 1868 the elite companies were merged with the fusilier companies and the collar badges were removed and all infantry adopted the red epaulettes. Nearly all the French foot troops and many of the mounted men wore a neck scarf, like a stock, but generally of mid-blue material. Officers had a black silk neck scarf. Two tunics had been issued to each man, one for parade and battle dress and the other for day-to-day wear, but before the war the second tunic was dispensed with, and field dress was authorised as the greatcoat worn over the waistcoat ('*veste*'). Officers were meant to wear the tunic in the field so that they could be easily recognised, as were sergeant-majors. However, many officers wore the greatcoat, especially in inclement weather.

French prisoners arriving in Germany by train.

Shako

The Model 1860 shako had a black leather body with black leather bands and chin strap. It carried a large brass eagle plate with the regimental number cut-out of a 'bomb' at the base. In addition to the cockade, it carried a small plume in full dress. It was replaced by the new Model 1867 which had a stiffened red felt body with yellow piping and a 35mm-wide blue band round the bottom edge with a yellow cloth regimental number. Above the band was a metal cockade, from the outside, red/white/blue with a brass button on the centre, from which a yellow cord loop ran to the top of the shako which carried a double red pompon. The shako had a black leather peak and chin strap, and was conical in shape, 115mm high at the front and 140mm down the sloping back. It had a small ventilation hole either side of the body. Some uniform items were not replaced immediately but were allowed to wear out. Hence many infantrymen still wore the black shako in the early months of the war. The new shako had an official life of four years.

Kepi

The item most associated with the French Army, referred to officially as the '*bonnet de police* with 'peak', was that most copied item of uniform, commonly called the 'kepi'. This small cap had a red top, a blue band bearing the number of the regiment in red, a black leather peak but no chin strap. The infantryman's cap had blue piping round the top and on the front and side seems. The officer's kepi was the same, but the piping was in gold. The number of gilt piping bands increased with rank, a lieutenant one or two rows, a captain three rows and a *chef de bataillon* four rows. All officers had a false chin strap behind the peak also in gilt. On the crown of the cap, officers had a large Hungarian knot also with the number of piping bands increasing in number denoting the rank of the wearer.

Veste and Trousers

Each soldier had a '*veste*', a waist-length sleeved waistcoat, which was single-breasted and closed by nine buttons, coloured plain dark blue with no decoration. It was usual on campaign to leave the tunic in the depot and just wear the waistcoat under the greatcoat. The plain red trousers were fitted at the waist and closed by a button fly and were supported by braces. They trousers were worn tucked into white or black gaiters.

Greatcoat

The greatcoat extended from neck to hem about 1,220cm [4 feet], was double-breasted and had two rows of six brass buttons. As with the tunic it had a small loop of material on the right-hand side of the waist secured by a button to support the waistbelt and equipment. A further small button was fixed just below the stand-up collar to attach the epaulette which was held in place with a blue cloth bridle. The back of the coat had a half belt to give a better fit and a button to secure the front of the coat when it was turned back for marching. Two small buttons were fitted above and below each cuff. The front of the collar had a small red three-pointed patch.

Pack

The cowhide pack contained the rest of the soldier's effects, either in it or on it: three shirts, a pair of shoes, hob-nailed and lace up, a pair of gaiters (if the soldier was wearing the white canvas ones, the black leather pair were carried in the pack), the neckcloth, a pair of underpants (long johns extending from waist to ankle), a pair of cotton gloves, a bag to hold the tunic when not being worn, two handkerchiefs, a clothes brush, a leather polishing brush, a flask and a bowl, and the soldier's record book. The French Army made good use of the handkerchief and printed on it all kinds of instructions to the soldier (such as how to lay out kit for inspection, the parts of the Chassepot and how to give first aid), all set out within coloured panels. The cavalry and artillery had their own designs.

Equipment

The black leather waistbelt was closed by a large brass plate at the front and supported a bayonet frog and a black leather ammunition pouch that contained three compartments for ammunition with a small expense pouch on the front of the belt. The pouches were fitted with loops so that they could be moved to any position comfortable to the wearer. Other essential pieces of kit were the linen bread-bag worn over the right shoulder and the water-bottle worn on the right hip. This was made of metal and covered in blue cloth. Strapped to the soldiers back was the haversack to which was attached sections of tent and tent poles and a cooking pot or mess tin. Not equipment as such, or uniform, was a large swathe of cloth worn around the waist, usually in a shade of blue, but could also be red or even green. This was not universal but was commonly worn by both officers and men.

Infantry Rank Badges

Rank and NCO distinctions was shown by diagonal strips of cloth set at an angle of 25 degrees just above the cuffs, a single yellow stripe for a 'Soldier First Class' (these were men from the former 'elite' companies, the grenadiers and *voltigeurs*), two yellow stripes for a corporal and a single gold stripe for a sergeant. The sergeant-major had two gold stripes. The stripes were 84mm wide on the tunic and 88mm wide on the greatcoat. The quartermaster's distinction, which could be awarded to corporals or sergeants, was a gold diagonal stripe worn on the upper arm. Long service stripes were worn on the upper arm in three grades in the form of inverted chevrons: one, two or three chevrons in red wool for seven, 14 and 21 years, respectively.

Chasseurs

The tunic issued to the *chasseurs* was similar to that of the line infantry, but with white metal buttons and epaulette straps and fringes in green with yellow half-moons. The cuffs were pointed instead of round as in the line. Trousers were bluey-grey with yellow piping down the outside seam, over which were worn white or black gaiters. The kepi was all blue with yellow piping and a yellow battalion number shown on the front. Officially the Model 1860 black shako should have been worn, but the troops discarded it in favour of the kepi. Another item of the 1860 uniform was the short tunic, known as the '*basquine*', which was favoured as a field dress. It was single-breasted and had the same colour and piping as the 1868 tunic, except that the piping went all round the skirts. *Chasseurs* also were issued with a sleeved waistcoat and greatcoat, which were supposed to constitute the field dress, but most troops appeared in tunics of various descriptions. Rank was as the line, but silver replaced gold. Equipment was the same as the line except for the belt buckle which resembled a double clip instead of a plate. Officers wore a similar uniform, but their tunics tended to be very dark blue.

The Army of Africa

Infantry

The *zouaves* of the line in 1870, like their compatriots in the Guard, were composed of Europeans, but still affected Arab-style dress. The *shama* and *veste* were dark blue with red braid, with the false pocket coloured to distinguish the three regiments, the 1st being red, the 2nd white and the 3rd yellow. The full-dress trousers were red with dark blue trim, the summer field dress trousers were plain white cotton with white gaiters and black shoes. It was the customary to wear a mid-blue sash or cummerbund around the waist with the black belt over it and the expense ammunition pouch at the front, over the belt buckle. Both the zouaves and the *turcos* had a short cape-like coat with a hood attached; for the zouaves it was dark blue grey and for the *turcos* sky-blue. The pack was carried on black shoulder straps and not hooked onto the belt. It was also the custom among North African units to pile up equipment on top of the pack rather than strap it to it. The *chechia* had a dark blue tassel. Officers had the same dress as the Guard regiment: in full dress a dark blue long tunic with gilt buttons and fringed epaulettes, in undress a similar tunic without the epaulettes and with rank shown by the Hungarian knots on the sleeves above the cuffs. The black waistbelt could be worn under or over the tunic, as could a mid-blue cummerbund. The kepi had a red top piped gold and a blue lower band and gold false chin strap.

French prisoners arriving in Germany.

As the zouaves eventually became a fully European force, North African native troops were absorbed into the *tirailleurs algériens*, or *turcos*. They were organised into three regiments the same as the zouaves. All the lower ranks were Algerian natives, as were the majority of the NCOs, and the officers up to lieutenant rank, while captains and above were Frenchmen. The style of the uniform was as the zouaves with a change of colour. A sky-blue *shama* and *veste* trimmed with yellow braid was worn with the regiment being shown by the colour of the false pocket. A white turban was exchanged for the *chechia* in parade dress. The cummerbund was usually crimson. The full-dress trousers were blue with yellow trim and plain white in summer. Native officers had the *shama*, *veste* and dress trousers trimmed with black silk decoration. They also had a gilt buckle on the black sword belt in addition to Algerian soft leather brown boots or European black leather boots. The basic colour of the European officer's tunic was sky-blue with a yellow collar and yellow piping round the pointed cuffs. In full dress gold epaulettes were worn with a gilt gorget. The field tunic had no epaulettes, rank being shown by the gold Hungarian knots on the sleeves. When the tunic was worn open it revealed a sky-blue *veste* with gilt buttons. A crimson cummerbund could be worn under or over the tunic. Baggy red trousers, tightening towards the ancles, with a sky-blue stripe and a black belt with gilt buckle as well as the kepi with a red top, piped in gold, with a sky-blue lower band and gilt false chin strap completed the uniform.

Marine Infantry

The marine infantry was under the control of the French Navy and were used as occupation troops in France's overseas colonies. They were not 'marines' in that they were not employed on board ship. They were nicknamed the '*marsouin*' ('porpoises'). In full dress they had a blue double-breasted tunic with red piping around the collar and pointed cuffs and two rows of eight yellow metal buttons, along with yellow fringed epaulettes. A small red anchor cloth badge was worn on either side of the collar. Two small buttons were on the cuffs, one below the piping and the other above. Dark blue grey trousers with a broad red stripe, white gaiters and black shoes were worn. The belt and pack straps were white, and the brass belt buckle had an embossed anchor. The marine infantry wore a black shako with yellow lace round the top and in a 'V' at each side. A double yellow pompon adorned the tricolour cockade as well as an imperial eagle plate. The brass chin scale was worn above the peak and a black leather strap under the chin. In field dress the *veste* was worn with the dark blue greatcoat, which was double-breasted and had a red three-pointed tab on each side of the collar. The field dress trousers had a thin red piping on the outside seams. The belts and straps were black. The kepi was entirely dark blue with red piping. Officers wore a very dark blue tunic with gold buttons and small gold anchors on the collar, along with dark blue grey trousers piped red tucked into high black or brown boots.

The *Régiment Étranger* (Foreign Legion)

The Foreign Legion regiment consisted of four battalions and was based in North Africa. It recruited widely, from France and in fact from anywhere. There were a number of Germans in its ranks, and it was thought politically insensitive to bring them to France. However, many were from the former kingdom of Hanover and were more anti-Prussian than the French native troops! They stayed in Algeria, although a fifth battalion was later raised in Paris. The uniform of the regiment was the standard infantry dress with a blue patch on the greatcoat collar and green epaulets and fringes with red half-moons. The infantry kepi had a red five-pointed star on the front in place of the regimental number.

Cavalry of the Line

The French cavalry was divided into three types: reserve, line and light. The reserve cavalry consisted of cuirassiers, that of the line of dragoons and lancers, and the light of hussars and *chasseurs*. The so-called 'African' cavalry was considered light. Each branch supposedly had a function: shock for the first, general service including dismounted operations for the second and reconnaissance for the third.

The French cavalry still lived in the era of decisive charges which led to the disasters of Morsbronn, Froeschwiller and Sedan. It had neglected its main tasks of reconnaissance – finding the enemy's dispositions and denying the gathering of information by the enemy. In 1868, a ministerial report suggested that a Prussian-style line or light cavalry regiment be made available to each infantry division, but the project failed. However, a cavalry division was attached to each corps in addition to the three independent divisions. During the short campaign leading to Sedan, the infantry was disconcerted that their movements were being discovered by German cavalry patrols while seemingly theirs did nothing to prevent it. The French cavalry doctrine considered shock action as their role even if practice showed the opposite. The 4th and 5th squadrons of the 12th Dragoons dismounted at the village of Forbach during the battle at Spicheren and fought off the Prussian advance using their Chassepots!

The cavalry of the line was made up of ten regiments of cuirassiers, 12 of dragoons, eight of lancers, 12 of *chasseurs* and eight of hussars. The reserve and line regiments had five squadrons, six for the *chasseurs* and hussars. One squadron per regiment remained behind as the depot, to train and organise replacements for the field squadrons. All French cavalry was to adopt a new tunic from 1867, but only the cuirassiers seemed to have changed completely. In the field many men adopted a more comfortable dress; officers in particular took to wearing a kepi and most troopers added the universal water-bottle, in a blue cloth cover, on a black strap, over the right shoulder and resting on the left hip. The cavalry of the line was issued a special greatcoat (mantle), which was a fairly voluminous coat with a large collar and a cape with a slit up the rear skirts to facilitate use on horseback, which could be closed with buttons. It had cloth covered buttons down the front of the coat and further buttons for the cape. The coat had deep cuffs and a large square pocket on either side, with a half belt at the rear. The colour generally was a light blue-grey and is described as such, but the actual material was '*blanc piqué de bleu*', white cloth with blue threads.

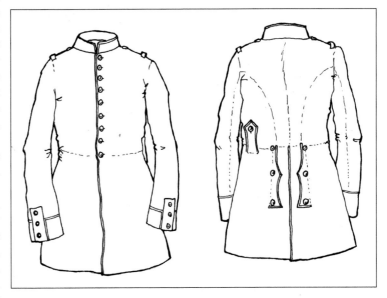

French tunic for heavy cavalry, front and back views.

The Cuirassiers

Six of the ten cuirassier regiments were part of the reserve cavalry and four were with the 1st and 6th corps. The Michel Brigade was massacred in the narrow village streets of Morsbronn and the four regiments of Bonnemains reserve division were also massacred by Prussian infantry and artillery at Frœschwiller. The cuirassiers wore the same uniform as the Guard cuirassiers, the regiments distinguished by the numbers on the white metal buttons as well as red epaulettes in place of the Guard's white. The steel helmet had a band of black sealskin covering the lower part of the skull and the front visor. Arms were the three-bar brass hilted sword and the Model 1822 pistol, converted to percussion in 1857, with a steel barrel and brass fittings. Officers had red trousers with a broad blue stripe and knee-high boots. White metal parts were silvered, and brass parts gilded.

The Dragoons

Ten dragoon regiments participated at the start of the campaign. Only the 6th arrived after the start of hostilities. The 3rd regiment was involved in a tragic error at the battle of Mars-la-Tour where they mistook the Guard lancers for enemy dragoons causing a number of casualties. Whereas the cuirassiers had been issued with the new uniform, the dragoons had begun to change over in 1867, but by 1870 the change was still incomplete. Some units took the field wearing the old uniform. The regiments wore a green single-breasted coatee with different coloured plastrons, collars and cuffs and cuff flaps. For undress a green plastron was worn in place of the coloured full-dress item. All troops wore red epaulettes and red riding trousers for mounted duties and red trousers over the short boots for foot duties, both with green piping. The helmet was the same pattern as the cuirassiers, but made entirely of brass, with a band of imitation leopard skin, black horsehair mane and a black tuft. For parade dress a squadron pompon and red plume were added. The helmet was issued with a cloth cover that was worn in the field. The waistbelt and sword slings were white as was the pouch belt, which carried a small brass grenade badge on the flap. The short turn-backs had a cloth grenade badge and piping in the facing colour. The regiments numbered 1 to 4 had a white plastron, numbers 5 to 8 yellow and 9 to 12 red.

Regiment	Collar	Cuffs	Cuff flaps
1	White	Green	White
2	White	White	Green
3	Green	Green	White
4	Green	White	Green
5	Yellow	Green	Yellow
6	Yellow	Yellow	Green
7	Green	Green	Yellow
8	Green	Yellow	Green
9	Red	Green	Red
10	Red	Red	Green
11	Green	Green	Red
12	Green	Red	Green

All facings were piped in the opposite colour.

French dragoon in greatcoat.

The new uniform was a blue tunic with a white collar piped blue, blue cuffs, piped white and white piping down the front. When mounted the rear tails could be turned back revealing the red lining. The dragoons carried the Model 1854 sabre and carried a Chassepot carbine. Officers wore the old or new uniform depending on whether their regiment had adopted the blue tunic. In either case they had gold epaulettes, gilded buttons and helmets. White belts were replaced by black in the field. The kepi had a red top, with, in the old uniform, a green lower part piped gold with a gold false chin strap and gold grenade badge on the front. The new kepi had a dark blue lower part in place of the green. Red trousers with broad green or blue stripes and a variety of different footwear, from knee high boots to black leather gaiters, completed the outfit.

The Lancers

In 1870 all eight regiments of lancers took the field. Two squadrons of the 6th charged with the Michel Brigade at Morsbronn, the 3rd took part in the charge of the cuirassiers at Rezonville and Sedan. The 1st and the 7th regiments were badly shot up. Some of the 2nd and 6th escaped the German net and later joined the Army of the new Republic. The lancers were also in the process of being outfitted with the new tunic, but many still wore the old uniform in 1870. The coatee was dark blue with blue pointed cuffs, white belts and epaulettes and white metal buttons. The belt had a square brass buckle with a crossed lances motif. Red riding trousers with leather false boots were worn. The shapka had a blue top, a white band and black leather skull. On the front a large brass plate with the number of the regiment appeared in white metal. The peak was also edged with brass. The chin chain was hooked up on the right-hand top corner. For parade dress a hanging plume of red horsehair was worn on the left side. The sabre was the light cavalry model of 1822 and the lance was black-painted wood with a steel butt and point and a white-over-red pennon; troopers also carried a percussion pistol. Officers had the same dress with silver and gilt replacing the white metal and brass of the troopers. The waist and pouch belt were silver with three blue velvet stripes. The long red trousers had a broad blue stripe down the outside seams. Regimental distinctions were yellow plastron and coatee tails for the first four regiments and red for the remaining four. In the field all ranks wore their shapka in a black oilskin cover and officers exchanged the belts for plain black leather.

Regiment	Collar	Cuffs
1	Yellow	Blue
2	Yellow	Yellow
3	Blue	Blue
4	Blue	Yellow
5	Red	Blue
6	Red	Red
7	Blue	Blue
8	Blue	Red

Collar and cuffs were piped in the opposite colour. The new tunic was dark blue with yellow piping down the front, yellow collar and cuff flaps, blue cuffs, white buttons and epaulettes. There is evidence that some squadrons removed their epaulettes in the field and wore a red-topped kepi with a blue band. Officers covered their pouch belts with a red leather sleeve.

The Hussars

Eight regiments of hussars remained at the start of hostilities. A ninth regiment had been dissolved in 1856 to supply the Guard regiments. The 2nd and 7th were in action at Mars-la-Tour and the 1st at the Battle of Sedan. Only the 3rd evaded capture. The 8th was stationed in Algeria and the 6th were garrisoned in Lyon and took no part at the beginning of the war. As with the rest of the cavalry the hussars were being issued new uniforms based on the tunic. However, only two regiments (the 1st and 8th) had been re-equipped by the time hostilities broke out, and the remainder either wore their old dress, or combinations of old and new. The hussar uniform adopted in 1860 was a dolman and pelisse in regimental colour: 1st sky-blue; 2nd chestnut brown; 3rd, silver grey (a pale blue); 4th, silver grey; 5th, dark blue; 6th, green; 7th, green; and 8th, sky-blue. The dolman had 18 rows of coloured braid across the chest, each with white metal buttons, one row to close the garment and a button at the end of each row (the 7th had brass buttons). All regiments had red collars and pointed cuffs edged with white lace, which also extended round the waist and the rear seams (orange yellow for the 4th and yellow for the 7th). Red riding trousers for troopers with a double stripe down the outside seams in the lace colour. The pelisse had six rows of hussar braid and a black fur edging to collar and cuffs, down the front edge and round the skirts. Arms were a light cavalry sabre and a Chassepot carbine. Sword and pouch belts were made of white leather. Headgear was a black fur busby with brass chin scales and a pompon in the squadron colour. In parade dress a red-over-white plume was added and the red bag with white piping was worn hanging down the left side. The dress sabretache was black leather with a yellow metal imperial eagle plate. A regimental-coloured stable jacket (veste) had a single row of nine buttons and a red tab on each side of the collar. Officer's braid and lace was black, and buttons silvered. They had a shako with a cardboard frame covered in oilskin and a silver pompon as field dress, but many officers and troopers had the Model 1868 kepi with a red top, piped blue, silver for officers, with a blue band with white, silver for officers, decorative piping knots. The 1868 uniform was a sky-blue tunic with red-pointed cuffs edged with white lace, with red piping round the collar and down the front. It had six white metal buttons each with hussar-type braid across the chest, white piping on the back seams and tunic rear vents. White cord epaulettes were worn on the shoulders. The busby, belts and arms were not changed. The red riding trousers now had a broad blue stripe down the outside seam. The trooper's stable jacket was now blue. The officer's tunic was all blue, the collar piped red and the cuffs with black lace. The braid was black. and the pouch belt was made of black leather. Trousers had a double silver stripe. Some troops kept their old pelisse. Officers could wear the busby with a silver pompon and silver piping as well as the shako in undress.

French Hussar Tunic, front and back views.

The *Chasseurs à Cheval*

Twelve regiments of *chasseurs à cheval* were listed in the order of battle. The 7th and 8th were taken from the various corps of the army at Sedan and were added to the new 12th Corps. The 11th was the only regiment to avoid capture. As with other branches of the cavalry a new uniform was proposed in 1868 and some men received it before the war broke out, or at least the 1st, half a squadron of the 6th and the 9th. Most regiments started out in July 1870 in the uniform authorised in 1854, which consisted of a green dolman with 18 rows of black wool braid and three rows of white metal buttons, a white waistbelt (worn underneath the dolman) and a pouch belt. Red riding trousers with double green stripe were also worn. The cap was a small black lamb's wool headdress, possibly based on a Turkish original and termed a '*talpack*'. It had a leather chin strap covered with a yellow metal chain and a rosette in the squadron colour at top centre which bore a small metal number of the regiment. A red-over-green plume was fitted for parade dress and a red bag hung on the left side which was piped white. The *talpack* had a white retaining cord at the back which looped round the neck and tied in front. The sword belt and slings and pouch belt were white. The black leather sabretache had a yellow metal imperial eagle. Arms were the 1822 light cavalry sabre and a pistol; however, the pistol was given up when the troops were issued with the Chassepot cavalry carbine. Officers had the same uniform with black silk braid, black lace edging to the collar and cuffs and black leather belts and straps. For parade dress there was a silver pouch belt with three red lines and a crown and chains on the chest, while for field dress, there was a black pouch belt, or a black cover with silver studs. They had the red riding trousers with double black silk stripes. Alternatively, red trousers were worn over short boots, or tucked into black or brown knee-high riding boots.

The new uniform authorised in 1868 was a sky-blue tunic with six white metal buttons each with a black hussar braid. The sky-blue collar was piped red, which continued down the front of the tunic. Sky-blue cuffs with black braid edging and red riding trousers with a broad sky-blue stripe were supplied. The *talpack* remained the same for officers and men with the alternative of a kepi with a red top, piped blue, sky-blue band with a red hunting horn badge, silver piping and badge for officers. In parade dress the officer's *talpack* had a red-over-green plume. Officers generally wore red trousers, either long for duties on foot, or tucked into knee-length riding boots for mounted duties. There was some latitude allowed in dress and an illustration shows an officer in a sky-blue waistcoat, closed by a dozen or more silver buttons, worn beneath a sky-blue pelisse with six hussar-type loops and black fur showing at the collar, cuffs and the front edges.

The Cavalry of the Army of Africa

The *Chasseurs d'Afrique*

In 1870 there were four regiments of *chasseurs d'Afrique*, each comprised of six squadrons. As the squadron pompons only amounted to five, an extra one had to be added, in this case, coloured orange. The *chasseur d'Afrique*'s uniform worn in 1870 had been introduced in 1862. It consisted of an officially sky-blue dolman, but depictions show a more mid-blue shade, with six woollen braid loops across the chest with three rows of white metal buttons. It had a yellow collar with black braid and blue cuffs piped black. Red riding trousers piped blue were worn. The full-dress red shako ('*casquette*') had a blue lower band and piping, with a national cockade with a blue loop, a squadron-coloured cockade and a small brass regimental number beneath the cockade. The shako sported a black leather peak and chin strap. It also had a black cord extending from the back of the shako body, round the wearer's neck across the chest ending in black flounders and tassels attached to a button on the left breast. A white pouch and waistbelt were also worn. Arms were the Model 1822 light cavalry sabre and a Chassepot carbine. Stable dress, which was worn on campaign, was a single-breasted *veste* with a yellow three-pointed collar patch. The stable dress cap was a red fez with a tassel in the squadron colour and black stripes around the base, one for the 1st Regiment and then up to four for the 4th Regiment. Riding trousers were red. Officers had the same uniform, but with black silk braid and silver buttons. The dolman had further black embellishments between the braid. Rank was shown by silver Hungarian knots on the sleeves. The red riding trousers were worn with double blue stripes on the outside seams. Some regiments (the 3rd and 4th) preferred knee-high riding boots. The kepi had a red top with a sky-blue band with silver piping and silver false chin strap. A pouch belt and sword belt of black leather with a gilded buckle completed the uniform.

The *Spahis*

Recruited from the native population of Algeria, three regiments of *spahis* existed in 1870. The proportion of native and Europeans was the same as in the *turcos* regiments. The trooper's *shama* was red with sky-blue piping around the edges and false pockets in the regimental colour: dark blue for the 1st, yellow for the 2nd and red for the 3rd. There was black braid on the front and around the sky-blue pointed cuffs. The sky-blue trousers were worn very full in the Turkish style. The troops did not have a mantle, but instead wore a white coarse cotton *burnous* (cape) with a second *burnous* in red over it. The *veste* was sky-blue with black braid worn under a red sash. A white cloth was worn below the waist tied to a strip of material which was fixed to the left shoulder. It is difficult to see its function, but possibly it was to protect the trousers from rubbing against the saddle. Arab soft leather brown boots were worn, while the headgear consisted of a white cotton scarf worn around the head secured by strip of brown camel hair; alternatively, there was a red fez with a blue tassel and a white turban. Weapons were the same as those of the *chasseurs*. Algerian officers wore a similar uniform, with black silk braiding and gold Hungarian knots on the sleeves. The camel hair that held the head scarf was intertwined with gold threads. French officers adopted a red dolman with red collar and sky-blue cuffs, black silk edging and six rows of braid. Black toggles closed the dolman and black rosettes were at the end of each braid. Gold Hungarian knots above the cuffs denoted rank. Trousers were sky-blue with a broad red stripe down the outer seams. A red sash with gold knots and red tassels was also worn. The kepi was sky-blue with gold lace and a gold false chin strap.

Cavalry Rank Distinctions

In cavalry regiments with square-cut cuffs the markings were the same as the infantry. Where the regiments had pointed cuffs, the marks were in the form of inverted chevrons, two red chevrons for a corporal (confusedly for English speakers known as a '*brigadier*' in French), sergeant (*marechal de logis*) a silver or gold chevron, depending on the button colour, sergeant-major (*marechal de logis chef*), two metallic chevrons and a warrant officer (*adjutant*), three. For officers the marks of rank were indicated by thin lines of metallic braid, the colour depending on the regiment's buttons, above the cuffs and extending above the elbow, almost to the shoulder. They were arranged in Hungarian-style loops and knots finishing with a point. The ranks are given their French names: *sous lieutenant*, one line; *lieutenant*, two lines; *capitaine en second*, three lines; *capitaine en premier*, three lines; *capitaine instructeur*, two lines in the opposite colour to the buttons and one in the button colour between them; *capitaine adjutant-major*, two lines in the button colour with one line not in the button colour between them; *chef d'escadrons*, three lines in the button colour and a fourth on the outside in the opposite colour; *major*, four lines; *lieutenant-colonel*, five lines with colours alternating; and *colonel*, five lines.

Other Line Troops

The Remount Depots

As the name implies the depots were set up to supply the army with horses, there were five depots in France and three in Algeria. The compliment was five senior veterinarians ranked as generals and 380 military veterinarians plus rank-and-file. The personnel wore a cavalry uniform of a dark blue hussar-style dolman with six rows of white braid across the chest, broad white lace around the collar and cuffs and on the rear seams, three rows of pewter buttons, and red riding trousers with a dark blue stripe. Full dress headgear was a shako the same as the *chasseurs d'Afrique*, with a dark blue pompon and a small white metal company number below the cockade. The undress kepi had a red top, piped blue and dark blue lower band.

Artillery

There were 20 artillery regiments of artillery: 15 regiments were numbered 1 to 15; one pontoon regiment was numbered 16; and four mounted regiments were numbered 17 to 20. Each foot regiment had 12 batteries and only eight were deployed in the field. The mounted regiments had eight batteries all deployed in the field. The pontoon regiment had 14 companies. At the beginning of the war five batteries were still in Algeria, and two in Rome as part of the French Army protecting the papal territories. The artillery numbered 30,000 men and 16,000 horses. The two Train regiments of 16 companies each were responsible for keeping the guns supplied with ammunition and equipment. There were also ten companies of sappers and six of pyrotechnicians. The mobilisation having been catastrophic, the regiments found themselves dispersed between each corps. For example, the 17th Horse Artillery Regiment had to divide its batteries between 2nd, 3rd and 4th Corps, and the 6th Regiment was divided between 1st, 5th and 7th Corps. The lack of a reserve Grand Park limited each gun to 440 rounds. In addition, the largest pieces were in the reserves.

The full-dress uniform of the foot gunners was a dark blue coatee with very short tails. The collar was blue piped red, with the pointed cuffs in red. The short tails were turned back red with blue cloth grenades and red piping on the false pocket flaps. A dark blue plastron front, piped red with two brass buttons just below the shoulders and a row of six buttons each side, finished at the waist. A small button was at the back of each cuff, three buttons on each pocket flap and two further buttons in the small of the back. Red-fringed epaulettes were on the shoulders. Blue trousers with a double red stripe, white gaiters and black shoes were also part of the uniform. The Model 1860 shako was black leather, with a copper flaming bomb device on the front and the regimental number as a cut out on the bomb. Under the bomb was a pair of crossed cannon barrels. Above the devise was a pressed metal tricolour cockade and above that a red woollen pompon. Attached to a hook at the back of the shako were a pair of red woollen cords which were tied around the neck and then fixed to the right epaulette and finished in red flounders and tassels. In parade dress a red horsehair falling plume was fitted behind the pompon. The chin strap was black leather. A white waistbelt was worn beneath the coatee to carry the bayonet frog. A white shoulder belt carried the black pouch, which had a small copper bomb and crossed cannon barrels on the flap. The dark blue greatcoat was carried around three sides of a black-painted knapsack with pack straps. The mounted troops had the same uniform with the addition of the blue riding trousers and leather false boots. They were issued with a light cavalry sabre in place of the bayonet. The officer's uniform was the same style, but the basic colour was black, with gilt buttons and epaulettes and gold cords on the shako. Gold bridles were worn on the shoulders to retain the epaulettes and gold grenades on the turn-backs. There were also a black waist and shoulder belts. A red feather plume was worn for parade dress, while in undress the shako was covered in a black oilskin. Officers' kepis had rows of gold lace, depending on rank and a gold false chin strap.

In the field both foot and mounted gunners wore the single-breasted *veste* with brass buttons and a small red tab on the front of the collar. The pack was dispensed with, and the greatcoat worn across the shoulder. The kepi was blue with red piping and a cloth grenade badge on the front.

The Engineers

The companies that made up the three engineer regiments were distributed among the Army corps, but the mobilisation had been very haphazard. Some companies were at half strength, their equipment was lacking and there were not enough horses for the officers. Some of the drivers who manned the transport service had not even been trained to ride! One of the engineer companies had received training in telegraphy and managed to lay cables linking various headquarters around Metz in August.

The uniforms were a mixture of infantry and artillery dress with infantry tunics and greatcoats and artillery trousers and kepis. Although armed and equipped as infantry the troops carried picks and shovels as part of their equipment. The large ammunition pouch worn at the back had a bursting grenade badge on the flap and the belt buckle had an embossed design of a sapper's helmet and breast plate – items that were still used for protection in the trenches during siege work. Mounted troops had a single-breasted tunic with black collar patches and cuff flaps. Epaulettes, shako cords and belts were the same as the artillery and a Model 1829 light cavalry sabre was equipped. The officer's undress tunic was black with black velvet tabs, piped red on the collar. The gold buttons were stamped with the same design as the trooper's belt buckle.

The Train

The Train was the organisation that kept the army supplied in the field. The uniform of the corps was a blue single-breasted tunic with silver embroidery of acanthus leaves on the collar and cuffs. In full dress a black bicorne was worn, and in the field a red-topped kepi with black lower band with acanthus leaves embroidery. The clerical staff had a blue tunic with a red collar with one to four gold lace bars, depending on rank and a red-topped kepi with a gold star on the black band. The Train consisted of four companies of labourers and three Train regiments. Besides their transport duties they were responsible for carrying the

French engineers field telegraph wagon. (*Illustrirte Zeitung*)

Image of French engineers field telegraph wagon in more detail.

wounded from the field dressing stations (termed '*ambulances*') to hospital and looking after the regimental pay chests.

The troops of the Train wore a single-breasted coatee, with short tails; the official colour was iron grey, but examples appear a greyish blue. The front of the coatee, collar, cuffs, cuff flaps were piped red, and the turn-backs were iron grey also piped red. The epaulettes and grenades on the turn-backs were red. There was red piping around the false pockets. Buttons were silver, with nine down the front of the coatee, three on each cuff flap, three on each false pocket and two in the small of the back. One button on each shoulder was used to secure the epaulette, which had a red loop to hold it in place. Mounted troops had red riding trousers with black false boots with a blue stripe. Drivers and non-mounted troops had red trousers with a red stripe, white gaiters and black shoes. In the field the undress *veste* with no tails was worn in colours the same as the coatee with the addition of three-pointed red tabs on the collar. White pouch belt, black pouch, white belt and sword slings and steel scabbard for the light cavalry sabre were standard. The kepi had a red top piped iron grey, an iron-grey band with a red grenade badge. Officers had the same uniform with silver epaulettes and buttons, and red trousers with a blue stripe. They retained the artillery shako for full dress, with silver bands at the top and sides and a gilded eagle plate and a silver rosette. A red falling plume was worn for parade dress.

The Intendency (Quartermaster Corps)

The Quartermaster Corps had responsibility for forage, general supplies, clothing, camp equipment and the Medical Corps. It was basically a civilian organisation consisting of 264 civil servants who were given positions analogous to military ranks, from captain up to general of brigade, including eight general inspectors, 26 military intendants, 150 sub-intendants and 80 assistants. They were given a uniform, but to distinguish them from the regular soldiers they were not permitted to sport a moustache! The clerical work was carried out by administrative officers, also civilians. It numbered 1,240 men in four offices, the offices of the quartermaster, the hospitals, supply and clothing. The uniform was a blue tunic with the collar and cuffs decorated with embroidery of gold acanthus leaves as was the black band of the red-topped kepi. The administrative officers had a blue tunic with a red collar with a gold lace bars on a black patch. Their kepi had a red top with gold lace and gold embroidered star on the black band.

The Medical Corps

The Medical Corps had 1,277 military doctors, including seven inspectors (generals), 390 majors, 800 assistants and 162 pharmacists. Each regiment included two doctors and an aide major. However, this number was woefully inadequate for the huge numbers of casualties suffered by both sides in the opening weeks of the war. Those wounded who survived the field *ambulances* (front-line hospitals) were then sent back to base hospitals to be treated by the non-regimental medical officers. The difficulties the regimental doctors faced is summed up in a contemporary report emphasising the lack of trained medical officers: 'The most basic dressing of an injured person requires an average of at least ten minutes; it will therefore take an hour to dress six wounded and ten hours for 60 wounded, assuming that a doctor can withstand the intolerable fatigue caused by the painful attitude he has to adopt to dress an injured person lying on the ground.'

Doctors wore a single-breasted dark blue tunic, without piping, with red collar and cuffs with gold embroidery for doctors and green for pharmacists. The embroidery was a curious mixture of oak and laurel leaves with a twisted snake running through it. The gold lace had tiny gold sequins sewn along its length. Red trousers, without any piping or stripes, generally tucked into high riding boots. The kepi had a red top and dark blue band with gold cords and sequins separating the two. On the band there was an emblem of oak and laurel leaves, with more sequins, and in the centre a medical symbol, the rod of Asklepios (ancient Greek god of medicine and healing) with a single snake entwined around the rod which was topped by a representation of a mirror (the 'mirror of prudence', which the French authorities declared all medical men need in abundance!). On the black leather peak lay a gold false chin strap. A black waistbelt supported an epee-type sword in a black leather scabbard with brass heel. Over the right shoulder was an officer's pouch belt covered in red leather and secured by gilt buttons. Doctors wore red cloth shoulder straps with gold lace, but no epaulettes. In the field medical orderlies wore an infantry blue greatcoat with two rows of white metal buttons and a red three-pointed tab on the collar. The epaulettes had red straps and pads and white fringes. They also had red trousers without stripes or piping, white gaiters and black shoes, and a black leather waistbelt and pack straps, without the ammunition pouches. The kepi was the infantry model with red top, blue band and piping. A red cross brassard was worn on the upper left arm. Like their Prussian counterparts, the idea of non-combatant status was not fully accepted, and orderlies were armed with an infantry sidearm and a carbine.

The Standards

The imperial eagle and commemorative battle names were reinstated in 1851. The standards were 90cm^2 and carried on the obverse the inscription 'Louis Napoléon au ...' and the letters 'LN' and 'RF' at the corners. In 1854, the silks sheets of the 1851 standards were disposed of and replaced by new ones taking the model of the 1812 design with the same embroidery, the inscription 'L'EMPEREUR NAPOLEON III AU (name and number of unit) ...' on the obverse and the names of victories gained from 1792 on the reverse. All decoration was in gold wire and thread, and the sheet was fringed in gold. The silk fabric of the standards deteriorated, and replacements were issued between 1861 and 1869. The eagles were made from aluminium and gilded. The plinth on which they were fixed had the number of the unit on the front and the type of unit (for example, 'INFANTERIE') on the back. Cavalry standards had the same design with the sheet measuring 60cm^2. The line infantry standard was carried by the 2nd battalion, while the 1st and 3rd carried a 50mm^2 marker flag, or 'porte fanion', crimson for the 1st and yellow and white divided diagonally for the 3rd.

French Line Infantry officer with eagle and standard.

The company fanions for the *turcos* were 40x30mm and followed this system, with the regulations of 1857 having laid down the colours: 1st battalion of each regiment: blue sheet; 2nd battalion: red sheet; 3rd battalion: yellow sheet; and 4th battalion: green sheet.

The devices were coloured by company (companies were numbered consecutively through the regiment and not the battalion): 1st, 5th, 9th, 13th: blue; 2nd, 6th, 10th, 14th: red; 3rd, 7th, 11th, 15th: yellow; and 4th, 8th, 12th, 16th: green

The *Garde Nationale Mobile*

The *Garde Mobile* was formed as a result of a programme of reform in 1868. The intention was to create a trained reserve to support the regular army in the field. However, while the organisation was proposed, little was actually done to train those men called to service. Lack of funds granted by the legislature was one reason and a lack of enthusiasm by the conservative military authorities another. Napoleon's power over the French population was slipping manifested by the downright antagonism of many of the men called to fill the ranks of the *Garde*. Marshall Niel's plan was that, after training, a force of 600,000 men would be available to support the regular army. However, it would take at least four years for these numbers to be assured. They were organised into companies and battalions and were to serve anywhere within the borders of France.

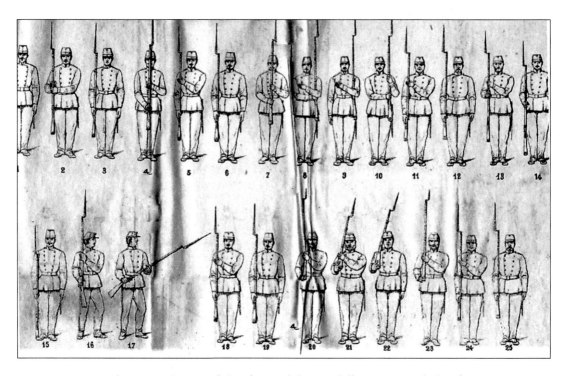

Page from a French National Guard manual showing drill movement with the rifle.

Many guardsmen were very politically aware and the Paris national guards, sent to the camp at Chalons, made their feelings quite plain. One wrote in his memoirs:

> As to discipline, we prided ourselves on ignoring the word altogether. We gave it clearly to be understood that we were not soldiers, but the Mobile National Guard. We expected to be treated with respect and to be commanded with politeness. Consequently, the most complete antagonism existed between the officers in command and the citizens they were endeavouring to convert into soldiers.

The *Garde Mobile* was a body made up of men aged 20–40, reservists from all regions who had not completed their military service but who were subject to periods of military training. It was hoped that should war break out they would be able to take on garrison and reserve duties and be able to fight alongside the regular troops. Count Palikao (general and for a short time, the last prime minister and minister of war under the empire) had called for the organization of 100,000 *Mobiles* in August 1870, which resulted in 400 battalions formed in the provinces with minimum training and equipment. On 29 August, 90 battalions were raised in Paris. Others were formed into mounted batteries, 12 of which were to be armed with the *Mitrailleuse*. Some mounted units were also created.

The *Mobiles* had a uniform similar to the line infantry, consisting of a double-breasted tunic, but with red collar and round cuffs and two rows of five brass buttons. Shoulder straps were blue with red piping. Trousers were dark blue grey with a broad red stripe down the outside seam, tucked into white or black gaiters. A blue kepi with a red band and piping and a tricolour cockade was standard, while fixed above the cockade was a red pompon with the regimental number in brass. Equipment was black leather identical to the line infantry. Officers had the same uniform, but with gold piping to the kepi and gold rank distinctions on the cuffs, braid or Hungarian knots. Officers generally wore boots, black or brown, marching or riding. This was the proscribed uniform, but in the field, it was a different matter and troops had to make do with whatever was available.

The *Garde Nationale*

The *Garde Nationale* (National Guard) had been a feature of the Revolution of 1789 and had been disbanded and reformed several times during the nineteenth century. There were two sub-divisions of the National Guard: the *Garde Nationale Mobilsee*, intended to act in the field in support of the Imperial Army; and the *Garde Nationale Sedentaire*, to be used for garrison and home duties. Camps were set up around the country to train the men. All men who were not part of the regular army or the *Garde Mobile* were expected to enrol. They were formed into companies, which were grouped together as battalions, three of which were formed into a '*légion*' or regiment. They were initially clothed, equipped and armed by their local departments.

The *Garde* was supposed to be dressed as the *Mobiles* but were at the bottom of the pecking order and clothing was supplied by the unit's local department, so it was a wonder that they got anything at all! They had tunics of local design and manufacture, trousers and kepis and a greatcoat if they were very lucky, but no red trousers as the military authorities did not want them mistaken for regulars!

Franc-tireurs

The origin of the *franc-tireurs* is somewhat obscure, as is the English translation of their name. The title 'Free Corps Volunteers' probably expresses the meaning as near as possible. Troops fighting in the irregular manner existed during the latter days of Napoleon I's empire when numbers of Germans, which ironically included a large contingent of Prussians, were formed during the 1813 and 1814 campaigns to attack retreating French units and disrupt their supply lines. They had little formal organisation and attacked against weak opposition and melted away against strong. Needless the say, the French took a dim view of these activities and were ruthless in dealing with them if caught. In 1867 the fear of war in Europe (over Belgium) raised feelings of patriotic fervour throughout France. Many towns and cities and workmen of all trades formed local shooting or gun clubs with the idea of supporting the regular authorities if needed. They were run by local committees or were under the patronage of a local personality. They paid for their own arms, anything from shotguns to modern Chassepots and everything in between. They enjoyed freedom from government officialdom and as a result devised many different styles of uniform, with each club having its own. Training was hit and miss, while some enthusiastically took to being 'soldiers' and achieved a high level of competence, many others were woefully inadequate. The clubs organised themselves and varied from the baron from the nearby chateau with 20 men from his estate to a large town that could field a couple of hundred well-armed and equipped men.

Soon after the war broke out the government tried to take over these groups and maintained a register at one time of over 70,000 officers and men. Some units were recognised as 'regular' troops by the French Republican government and incorporated into battalions and brigades, especially those units who joined Garibaldi's corps. Patrols, messengers and small posts being attacked by locals some of whom were manned by members of these clubs while others were from even more loosely formed groups. However, the Germans treated them all the same and if they were caught 'with weapons in their hands' and not wearing any uniforms, they were put up against the nearest wall. Later in the war, some *franc-tireur* units were brigaded with regular battalions and mobilised national guards and were issued with papers to say that they were regarded by the French government as 'regulars' and paid accordingly so as to avoid being shot out of hand by the Germans if captured.

Staff Corps

Created in 1818, the Staff Corps was a special arm, open to the best students from the Saint Cyr Academy who passed the competition of the Staff School. This school, which recruited sub-lieutenants, allowed the officers to return to the prestigious Staff Corps, which was composed of a fixed number of officers of each rank (in 1868, 580 officers, including 35 colonels, 35 lieutenant colonels, 110 squadron leaders, 300 captains and 100 lieutenants). After training in the different arms of the army for about 6–8 years, the staff officer, promoted to captain, was assigned to an existing staff or served as aide-de-camp to a general officer. The Staff Corps, although prestigious, was long criticized for training officers with poor knowledge of the troops. In addition, the failures of the Imperial Staff in 1870 highlighted the need to reform the institution and the training of officers. It was only in 1878/1880 that the reform was completed.

Schools

St Cyr

Created by Napoleon I, St Cyr was organized at Fontainebleau in 1803. In 1807 he wanted to restore the Palace of Fontainebleau for his personal use, and so he thought about transporting the school to another place. He settled on St Cyr and on 1 June 1808 the military special school was reopened in the royal property of Saint Louis, which had been founded in 1685 by Louis XIV in order to educate young girls of the poor nobility. The purpose of the special military school was to prepare the young men who were destined for military service as officers in the ranks of the army. Applicants were between 18 and 22 years old and had to pass an entrance examination. Admitted candidates are required to complete, before entering the school, a year of military service in a regiment under ordinary conditions. The duration of the courses at St Cyr was two years. The school, commanded by a general officer, assisted by a lieutenant colonel second-in-command, comprised a cadre of instructing officers and teaching officers. The pupils were expected to perfect their military training and received a general instruction consisting of various courses: tactics and military history, topography and geography, administration and legislation, professional ethics, artillery and fortification, drawing and German.

École Polytechnique

The *École Polytechnique*, established in Paris was intended to train its pupils for the services of the artillery (metropolitan or colonial), engineering, the police forces of the colonies, the navy and various public functions (bridges and roadways, mines, water and forests). The studies lasted for two years. The school was run by a general of brigade, seconded by a lieutenant colonel.

Cavalry Training School

The Cavalry Training School at Saumur was instituted to improve the training of lieutenants, complete that of the newly promoted sub-lieutenants, give men aspiring to be officers the general knowledge that every officer must possess and complete the technical instruction of the veterinary assistants. The course lasted for 11 months. The school was run by a colonel or a brigadier general. It was comprised of 40 lieutenants of instruction, detached from the cavalry regiments of the army (at the rate of one per brigade) to perfect themselves in the science of the horse, military work, tactics and all the questions concerning the cavalry. They were intended to carry their knowledge back to their regiments, most as instructor captains. Lieutenants of artillery attached to the school at the rate of one per brigade and followed the same courses in order to later become commanders of horse batteries. There were also 80 lieutenants (pupils) from the special military school at St Cyr; a section of 120 NCOs who were students of cavalry or artillery and followed the courses of one year at the end of which they were appointed sub-lieutenants; 25 trainee veterinary assistants who came for a one-year course before obtaining the rank of veterinary assistant; a division of dispatch riders (about 80 pupils) from the light cavalry regiments who followed a one-year course before returning to their units to form the dispatch section (six men per unit).

Prytannée Militaire de la Flêche

The *Prytannée Militaire de la Flêche* was intended for the sons of officers to provide them with an education that prepared them for a military career. A total of 438 residents, aged 9–18 years old, were kept at the school at state expense.

Guard of Paris

The Parisian police force (called the 'Guardians of Peace') was a civilian organisation responsible for keeping crime in check within the city. The government could also call upon the military if greater force was required. Between the two there was the *Garde de Paris*, a militarised police force, like the *Gendarmerie*, but only within the bounds of the city. Its origin was to be found in the *Garde Municipale de Paris* created by Napoleon I when First Consul in 1802, and through various titles to the Republican Guard constituted during the Revolution of 1848. (This ousted Louis Phillipe as king and first brought in the Second Republic with Prince Louis Napoleon as the democratically elected president from 1848 to 1851. This was followed by the *coup d'état* by Louis Napoleon, who created the Second Empire with himself as emperor.) The *Garde Municipale* could be called upon by the Prefect of Police and the Minister of the Interior to maintain order in the city. Its original complement was 2,200 infantry and 400 cavalry, made up of two battalions of infantry each of eight companies and four squadrons of cavalry quartered in various barracks throughout the city. The *Garde* formed part of the escort of Napoleon III during his visit to the opera on 14 January 1858, when Orsini and his fellow conspirators set off several bombs. Napoleon escaped unharmed, but two Guards were killed and 12 wounded. The *Garde Municipale* patrolled all public spaces and buildings in Paris, including theatres, barriers at the main gates, government offices, public gardens, and markets for meat and vegetables (this last called the 'service of the *petit pois*'!). The arms of the mounted troops consisted of the Model 1822 light cavalry sabre, the Model 1842 *Gendarmerie* carbine and the Model 1842 muzzle-loading pistol. The infantry carried the Model 1842 *Voltigeur* musket until 1869 when they were re-equipped with the Model 1866 breach-loading Chassepot rifle.

The mounted guards wore a steel helmet with a brass comb, with a red tuft or 'houpette' on the front of the comb and a red plume on the left side. There was a black horsehair mane falling from the back of the comb, a brass imperial eagle plate and black leather chin strap covered with a brass chain that was connected to large brass rosettes. The steel front and back peaks were edged with brass. The full dress 'habit' was a long-tailed coatee of dark blue with a plain blue collar and blue round cuffs and cuff patches, piped red. The tails were lined red with red turn-backs on which was sewn a red grenade badge on a blue patch. The horizontal pocket flaps were piped in red. On the front of the coatee was large plastron, double-sided, blue and red, secured by six buttons on each side and a single button on each side of the chest. There were three buttons on each pocket flap and two buttons at the rear as well as three small buttons on each cuff flap. A further button on either shoulder was used to secure the epaulettes. All buttons of brass, gilded for officers, were stamped with an eagle and the letters 'GARDE DE PARIS'. Red shoulder straps ended in a large trefoil and an aiguillette on the right side (sometimes on the left side, illustrations show either!). Red bridles were used to hold the straps. The undress coatee was single-breasted with a row of nine buttons, other details were the same as the full dress coatee. White gloves with gauntlet cuffs, white riding breeches and knee-high black boots as well as a black stock were also worn. A white belt over the right shoulder supported the black pouch. Guards were armed with the Model 1822 cavalry sabre with a white sword knot and the Model 1842 *Gendarmerie* carbine. NCOs had the epaulette strap, trefoil and aiguillette in alternate red and yellow colours. Officers had gilded epaulettes with fringes, gold aiguillette and a gold sword knot. For walking out dress the troopers replaced the helmet with a black bicorne and had blue trousers with a broad black stripe. The kepi had a blue top piped red with a black lower band with a red grenade badge on the lower band. The officers' kepi replaced the decoration with gold.

The guards on foot had a very similar uniform, but with a black shako decorated with red, edged yellow lace around the top and inverted 'V' shapes at each side; a brass eagle plate topped by a tricolour cockade and a double red pompon. A false chin scale of brass rested on the peak and there was a real chin strap of black leather. White cross belts supported a cartridge pouch and short sabre, with a brass plate on the sword belt. The blue trousers had a broad black stripe. Service dress was a double-breasted greatcoat with brass buttons and epaulettes and aiguillette. The shako had a black cover with a yellow grenade painted on the front. Barrack dress was a plain blue waistcoat and kepi.

The guard had a band of 61 officers and men, including the '*chef de musique*'. The musicians wore the same uniform as the guards, but with gold lace around the collar and cuffs.

Plate 1 French Line Infantryman, full dress

Plate 2 Prussia, Grenadier Regiment King Frederick William II (1st Silesian) No. 10 Parade dress

Plate 3 Prussian infantryman, fatigue or working dress

Plate 4 Prussian *Feldpost*, bugle held on a 'German' coloured cord, white/black/red

Plate 5 Prussia, NCO of stretcher bearer section

Plate 6 French 'Genie' engineer company corporal, working dress

Plates 7 and 8 France, dragoons, trooper new uniform and officer 3rd Regiment in pre-1868 uniform

Plate 9 Prussia, Jäger company, mounted soldier of the Train (supply) section

Plate 10 Hesse, 2nd Jäger Battalion, 4th company, identified by the sword knot

Plate 11 Saxon infantryman, Prussian helmet with Saxon plate, tunic with round cuffs and piping along the edge of the tunic

Plates 12 and 13 France, lancers, officer in pre-1868 full dress, trooper in campaign dress

Plate 14 France, infantry sapper, corporal with two long service chevrons

Plate 15 France, Sub-Lieutenant infantry field dress. Privately purchased pistol, small satchel and brown leather gloves

Plate 16 France, trooper of the Remount Service

Plate 17 France, trumpeter of the Carabineers, full dress

Plate 18 Bavaria, Engineer troops, private of the Telegraph Section, the railway section had the same uniform with a large 'E' (for *Eisenbahn*) in place of the 'T' on the right arm

Plate 19 Brunswick private of (Prussian) Infantry Regiment No. 92

Plate 20 Württemberg, Senior Lieutenant of the 4th Cavalry Regiment, 'Queen Olga' in full dress, wearing the cavalry shako and holding the *pickelhaube* introduced in 1869

Plate 21 France, *Fusilier Marin* **in naval 'pea coat'**

Plate 22 France, *Chasseur à Cheval*, uniform introduced in 1868, the tunic is cut at the sides and back to facilitate use mounted, the red lining to the skirts can just be seen

The *Garde* was called out, in May 1870, just before the outbreak of the war, to clear rioters who had built barricades near the centre of the city.

The Naval Infantry

Marines

Unlike several other maritime nations, France had no specific marine corps. In the French Navy, one of the specific grades was that of '*fusilier*' – that is, a sailor who had reached a standard of infantry proficiency. These sailors were used for relatively minor landing duties where no actual soldiers were available on-board ship. For major operations they were replaced by regular soldiers. They were not organised into battalions but were merely part of a ship's compliment. However, in 1870, immediately after the abandonment of any plans to land troops in Denmark and north Germany, they were withdrawn from the naval vessels and sent as ad hoc battalions to the field armies and especially to Paris to man the large guns that had been added to the defences. The army had raised infantry regiments to fight on ships and in the French colonial campaigns from the early 1600s, notably in America and in India. In 1831 two Marine regiments were raised, followed by a third. In 1870 they were quickly mobilised for land service and two brigades fought at Sedan in the defence of Bazeilles. Other marine battalions were raised as line infantry and sent to Paris and the various field armies.

Their headgear consisted of a dark blue kepi with red piping and a red anchor badge on the front. The double-breasted tunic was dark blue with yellow metal buttons and red piping down the front and on the pointed cuffs with a red anchor on either side of the collar. Yellow epaulettes were worn in full dress. The bluish-grey greatcoat sported yellow metal buttons, stamped with the regimental number and an anchor. A red cloth badge was situated on either side of the collar. Blue-grey trousers with a wide red stripe down the outside seam were worn most of the years, with white trousers in summer. Gaiters were black leather. The equipment was black leather with brass fittings and an anchor was stamped on the belt buckle. The officer's full-dress shako was of very dark blue, almost black cloth, braid, with side chevrons in gold and front plate and chin scales of gilt metal, complete with a yellow pompon. The officer's kepi had gold lace, chin strap and anchor badge. The tunic was similar to that of the troops with red piping and gold anchors on the collar, rank shown by gold lace in the form of Hungarian knots above the cuff, and gold epaulette bridles. The greatcoat had gold lace round the cuffs, a gold anchor on each side of the collar and gold epaulette bridles, with gold epaulettes in full dress. A waistbelt with black slings supporting a sword with a slightly curved blade in a steel scabbard with gilt hilt and sword knot. Officers wore white gloves.

The French Navy in 1870

In 1870 the French Navy was second only to the British naval forces. A ship-building and naval-harbour-building programme initiated by Napoleon III to defend and protect France's growing overseas empire had been the driving force for the expansion of the navy, although a direct challenge to England was only contemplated by the most extreme members of the naval establishment. Ship design followed developments in naval armaments and new methods of propulsion. As with any vessel constructed at great expense, it was not a static design, but updated as new developments were added to naval architecture and armaments. As an example, the *Hercule* was laid down in 1825 as a 100-gun line-of-battle ship, but only launched in 1836. She was constructed of wood, displaced over 4,400 tons and was powered by sail. In 1854 it was part of the squadron which visited Kiel in the Baltic and in 1860 was taken off the list of active warships. In

1875 it was converted to a prison ship at Brest and finally scrapped in 1882. The *Hercule* class of ships were modified to steam power and the number of guns reduced to 90.

The invention of the exploding shell gun, rather than just firing solid shot, by the French general Henri-Joseph Paixhans in 1823, revolutionised naval architecture. The shell fired at a ship would lodge or break through the wooden structure and then explode with devastating consequences. The French Navy began equipping its vessels with the new artillery from 1827. Ship designers countered the effects of the exploding shell by adding plates of iron to the sides of vessels in various combinations, with belts of various thicknesses and in different positions. This eventually led to ships with all-iron hulls.

By 1870 the French Navy had 501 ships in its inventory, of which 53 were ironclads with broadside batteries and nine were ironclad carrying their guns in turrets, or *barbettes*. As well as large vessels there was a class of iron-clad gunboats, carrying two guns each, which could be dismantled for transport overland or for storage. As the personnel for the navy were conscripted there was never a shortage of sailors to man the fleet. The total of 170,000 men was recorded, but only about 74,000 were employed. As a result, many men were detached as they were no longer required to man such a large fleet and a number of naval battalions were added to the strength of the French Army.

One of the leading French designers, Henri Dupuy de Lôme, was born into a naval family, studied iron shipbuilding and steam power in England. He returned to France and published a book on his recommendations in 1844. In 1847 he designed a new vessel, named *Le Napoleon*, which was the first steam-powered and screw-driven battleship. It was launched in 1850. The engines developed 960 horsepower, and it displaced 5,000 tons, carried 90 guns on two decks and could make a speed of over 13 knots. It used prodigious amounts of coal and could travel for nine days at full power and had three masts for auxiliary sails. In the politically sensitive period of the mid-nineteenth century, it originally was allocated the name *Prince de Joinville* (after the third son of King Louis Philippe) but after the fall of the Orleans dynasty it was quickly renamed *24 Fevrier* and in 1850 *Le Napoleon* in honour of the first Napoleon. A further eight ships of the same design followed. In 1857 Dupuy de Lôme also designed *La Glorie*, a wooden steam ship, but with iron protection for her sides. Four more soon followed. Dupuy de Lôme was active in the air as well as at sea, and in 1870 developed a navigable gas balloon: an elongated bag, pointed at each end, carrying a gondola with a large propeller at the back powered by 4–8 men. The war ended before further development could take place.

The French line of battle navy was made up of several different designs of warship. The largest class of 114 guns consisted of two ships, both laid down before 1815: the *Ville de Paris* and *the Louis XIV*. The *Hercule* class, mentioned above, were steam-powered with auxiliary sails and included ten further vessels. The *Suffren* class were 90-gun sailing ships converted to 80-gun steam-powered ships; there were 12 ships in this class (although one had been wrecked in 1859). There were two ships in the *Tourville* class carrying 80 guns. The *Napoleon* design of steam-powered ships spawned two sub-classes with eight ships in all each mounting 90 guns. The most powerful ship in the world, at the time of launching in 1855, was the 130-gun *Bretagne*, although by 1870 most of its guns had been removed and it was used as a training ship. After the line of battle type ship, France had more than 30 stream-powered frigates carrying from 29 to 40 guns each. The fleet of paddle-wheel steamers were out of date by 1870 and most had been taken out of service and broken up.

Full dress for naval officers consisted of a black bicorne hat with a gold strap to hold the national cockade, a double-breasted blue tailcoat with two rows of nine gilt buttons, blue trousers with gold stripes down the outside seam and black shoes. The collar and cuffs had gold embroidery, decorative foliage and anchors with epaulettes and epaulette bridles of gold. A gold and blue silk braided belt was worn over the tailcoat and supported a sword in a black leather scabbard with gilt fittings and a black silk sword knot. The coat was generally worn open at the neck, down to the third button, revealing a white shirt with fold-down collar and a black necktie. White gloves completed the outfit. Undress was the bicorne, a coat without braid, but with epaulettes and a black leather sword belt with an oval buckle. The coat was also worn open at the neck. Field dress was a blue peaked cap with gold lace around the lower portion, the number of lace stripes depending on rank, a double-breasted blue frock coat with two rows of buttons, but with no decoration except for gold stripes round the cuffs to denote rank and gold epaulette bridles. Officers on the staff could wear epaulettes, with their coat collar turned down. In summer, white trousers were worn.

First mates, equivalent to a sergeant-major in the army, had a double-breasted blue reefer jacket with two rows of yellow metal buttons and two yellow stripes above the cuffs to denote rank. They also wore the peaked cap without any decoration. Second mates wore the sergeant's single yellow strip above the cuffs and single-breasted pea jacket. Both NCOs wore the jacket open at the neck to reveal the shirt and tie. Second mates and below wore the sailor's beret with a blue top and a black band with ribbons extending down the back of the neck and a red pompon on top. The name of the ship was embroidered in yellow on the front of the ribbon. A thin white cord chin strap was worn over the top of the cap. The sailors' full dress was a blue blouse, open at the neck with a large separate pale-blue collar almost covering the shoulders and edged with three white lines. The open collar was white at the front showing the white and blue horizontal stripes of the *veste*. A black scarf was worn under the collar. Plain blue trousers were substituted with white ones for summer dress. A sailor's working dress was a white blouse with the collar and scarf and white trousers, black shoes, or even no shoes at all!

3

The Prussian (North German) Army

After the overthrow of Austria and her allies in 1866, Prussia entered conventions with the German states north of the River Main which formed the basis of the army of the North German Confederation. All the states were obliged to conform to Prussia's organisation of battalions and regiments, the hodgepodge of weaponry was replaced by the Dreyse needle-gun and even the soldier's uniforms were changed to Prussian patterns, although some minor variations were allowed, at least for a time. The south German states also brought their armies into the Prussian organisation, forming two Bavarian army corps, and a Baden and a Württemberg division.

The army of the North German Confederation consisted of 12 army corps of the Line numbered 1–12 and one of the Guard (the 12th Corps was the former army of Saxony). The corps, except the Guards, were each drawn from a particular district of Prussia. The Guards were recruited from all over the kingdom. Each corps had two divisions of infantry, one of cavalry, 16 batteries of artillery and a military train (the

A Prussian regiment leaving barracks led by its band. (*Illustrirte Zeitung*)

transport troops of the army). Each division comprised two brigades and each brigade, two regiments. Each regiment had three battalions. The battalions were distinguished as 1st *Musketier*, 2nd *Musketier* and the (3rd) Fusilier battalions in the infantry regiments; 1st and 2nd Grenadiers and 3rd Fusiliers in the grenadier regiments; and 1st, 2nd, and 3rd Fusiliers in the fusilier regiments. These names were based on historical functions and by 1870 they had no further significance.

Prussian infantry leaving for the seat of the war, writing last minute letters, stocking up with cigars, and carriages decorated with green boughs.

The regiment was commanded by a colonel assisted by a staff, and each battalion had a major and a staff of non-combatants, including a surgeon and paymaster. The four field companies each had a captain, a senior and a junior lieutenant and 250 NCOs and men. A depot company existed to provide training for recruits and to make up the field companies as necessary. A cavalry division had two brigades, each of two regiments. The regiment put four squadrons into the field and reserved a depot squadron as in the infantry. A cavalry squadron fielded five officers and 150 NCOs and men.

The infantry was composed of the following: Nine Prussian Guard regiments, 15 grenadier regiments (numbered 1–12, 89, 100, 101), 77 infantry regiments, (13–32, 41–72, 74–79, 81–85, 87 and 88, 91–96, 102–107), 13 fusilier regiments, (33–40, 73, 80, 86, 90 and 108). Altogether this was 114 regiments, all of three battalions, making a total of 342 battalions. In addition, there were four regiments from the state of Hesse (each of two battalions), a Prussian Guard *Jäger* battalion, a Prussian Guard *Schützen* battalion (originally Swiss troops from the canton of Neuchatel) and 16 *Jäger* battalions.

The cavalry was composed of the following: Two Guard cuirassier regiments and eight Line regiments; three Guard lancer regiments and 16 Line regiments, classed as 'heavy cavalry'; two Guard dragoon regiments and 19 Line regiments; and a Guard hussar regiment and 16 Line regiments. The 'heavy' regiments were formed into brigades and divisions, while many of the dragoon and hussar regiments were allotted to infantry divisions to be used as scouts or escorts.

In terms of artillery, each army corps had its own artillery regiment. Each regiment had three battalions of foot artillery and one battalion of horse artillery. A battalion consisted of two batteries termed 'light batteries' of 4-pounders (nominal, weight of shot nearly double) and two batteries termed 'heavy batteries' of 6-pounders (again, the actual weight of the shot was almost double). Each battery consisted of six guns. The horse artillery battalion had three batteries of 4-pounders. Every infantry division had its artillery battalion with the third battalion forming the corps artillery reserve. The horse artillery batteries were either part of the corps artillery reserve or attached to a cavalry division.

Added to each army corps were various supporting troops, pioneer battalions, bridging companies and military train battalions.

Infantry Uniforms

All clothing was approved by the Military Cabinet, who authorised the Military Clothing Commission to issue sealed patterns for use by private tailors, government factories and the regiments themselves. In the Prussian service the patterns were sent to the army corps who passed them on to their regiments. Cloth was delivered from the depots to individual battalions who had their own craftsmen to make up the uniforms. During their compulsory service the craftsmen formed a 'non-combatant' section whose function was tailoring, shoemaking and leather-working, instead of regular soldiering. As recruits were enrolled for their military service any men with the right trade or experience were allocated to this 'craftsmen' section. The work was overseen in each regiment by its own small version of the clothing commission. Each infantry regiment retained at its depot a craftsman company of one officer and 160 men; a cavalry regiment, 41 men; the staff of an artillery regiment, one officer and 161 men; and a pioneer battalion, 40 men. These men were given basic drill training for a few weeks but were not armed.

And they had many uniforms to make. Each infantry soldier had several sets of uniforms, which did not belong to the individual soldiers but were the property of his regiment. Under the eye of a senior

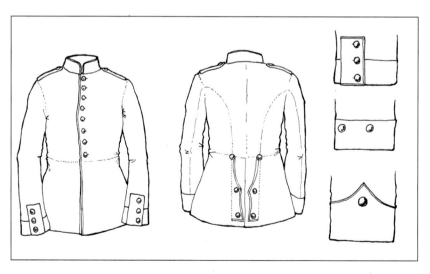

Prussian tunic, front and back views. Cuffs: top, Prussian, known as 'Brandenburg'; middle, square-cut, known as 'Swedish'; bottom, pointed, known as 'Polish'.

NCO was kept each man's newest, best dress, only issued for special parades or to be worn on campaign. A second uniform was kept for inspections and reviews, a third set for garrison guard duty, and the oldest set for daily duty, manoeuvres and so on. If a soldier had the money, he could have a uniform made by the battalion tailor or a civilian tailor for walking out (to the tavern at the weekend!). As an extra item, soldiers were issued with an off-white linen waist-length jacket for fatigue duties, exercises or general barrack wear. It was closed by a single row of tin plate buttons with hooks and eyes for closing the collar. It had a single button on each cuff and the jacket usually had a single breast pocket on the left side.

The *tunic* was introduced into the Prussian Army in 1842 and was dark blue for most infantry units and dark green for the *Jägers*. It was made of good quality thick woollen material and by 1870 was cut to fit the body. The sleeves and skirts were lined in blue linen and a lighter coloured lining was sewn into the chest. Eight buttons closed the front, from neck to waist, two buttons on the rear skirts, either side of a central vent, and a button on each shoulder to retain the strap. At the rear were two hooks shaped like buttons to give support to the waistbelt. In regiments with 'Brandenburg' cuffs (round cuffs with a cuff flap), there were three buttons on each cuff flap, while in regiments with 'Swedish' cuffs (plain round cuffs), there were two.

The Guards and Line infantry had red (called 'poppy red', which is a dull scarlet) collars and cuffs. Piping was also red down the left front of the tunic and the right front below the waist. There was also piping on the rear skirt flaps, which were a hangover from the skirt pocket flaps on the former tailcoats. The collar was closed with a hook and eye, under which the soldiers wore a black material stock closed at the back of the neck with a small buckle.

Officers wore a similar garment of superior quality material. It had a small opening on the left-hand side for the sword hilt, while the sword itself was carried on a leather belt beneath the tunic. It was a universal fashion for officers to leave the bottom button on the cuff flaps undone. As officers still wore epaulettes in full dress, there was small bridle on each shoulder to retain it, in gold or silver braid, edged in the colour of the regimental shoulder straps. Officers also wore black stocks, usually of silk.

Trousers issued to the infantry were black/grey woollen material with red piping down the outside seams. Just before the war a new pattern of trouser was introduced, which was dark blue with red piping. Very few troops wore the new pattern, mainly recruits and wartime volunteers. Both patterns had a least one pocket, buttoned flies and a rear waistband which could be tightened to fit. For parades, special duties and summer weekends trousers of plain white linen (the same as the grey trousers, but without the red piping) were authorised. An innovation was introduced in 1867 when underwear of grey calico, or old cut-up white linen trousers were issued. Before that date no underwear was issued, so those soldiers who wanted the garment had to buy it out of their pay. During the winter of 1870/71 the troops got woollen underwear. Officer's trousers were similar to those of the men, but with a tighter cut. The new dark blue pattern was not adopted until after the war. For mounted officers extra dark grey material or black leather was added to the inside of the legs. For parades white linen trousers were authorised and for gala dress, white cashmere (fine soft wool). All trousers supplied to officers had a small strap under the instep to keep them tight.

The item of uniform most often seen was the peak-less cloth cap, or *field cap*. Officially for use in garrison and undress, it became common during the campaign in place of the helmet. It consisted of a crown and a base, with the crown being slightly larger than the base. For the infantry the crown was dark blue with red piping (green for the *Jäger* battalions), the base had a red band with dark blue piping round the bottom of the band (green for *Jäger*). On the front of the red band was placed the state cockade, which was in the form of black/white/black rings for Prussia; the 93rd Anhalt Regiment had dark green; the 94th Saxe-Weimar, black/dark green/yellow; 95th Saxe-Coburg-Gotha, dark green/white/dark green; 96th (1st battalion) Saxe-Meiningen dark green/white/dark green, 2nd battalion the two Reuss principalities, black/red/yellow and the 3rd (fusilier battalion) Schwarzburg-Rudolstadt white/light blue/white. Any Prussian citizens serving in these regiments also had the black/white/black cockade above the band. Citizens of other north German states serving in Prussian regiments had their own state cockade placed above the band. A further cockade was in use for soldiers who had committed some minor indiscipline, but who stayed in the ranks; they were demoted to second-class soldiers and had the state cockade replaced by one of plain grey.

Corporals, sergeants and sergeant-majors and officer candidates wore a cap with a black patent leather peak. Sergeant-majors and officer candidates wore the state cockade, but in metal, black/silver/black for Prussia. The other states cockades changed white to silver metal and yellow to gold. Officers had a similar cap, although officially the crown was to be 2 inches (about 5cm) wider than the base and it was made from stiffer material. Reserve officers and those from *Landwehr* battalions added a small silver cross, shaped liked the Iron Cross medal to the band. Many officers had an informal cap for use on campaign, with or without the peak.

After the 1866 campaign against Austria a new model *footwear* was introduced. The old ankle-high boot was relegated to the soldier's pack and a new high boot was issued, reaching to the middle of the calf. It was intended that the trousers were to be tucked into the boots for most purposes. The boots had a loop on either side so they could be pulled on and the top made tight with a buckled tab. It was common for troops to be given boots one size too large to make them easier to break in with straw stuffed into the toes to make a good fit. Officers already had tall boots, almost reaching the knee. Mounted officers had screw-in spurs. During the war a black patent leather boot was authorised, similar to those worn in the cavalry, but not generally used.

Greatcoats could be worn in winter (officially November to March), if authorised by the regimental or battalion commander. Two models were in use: one introduced in 1832, and the other in 1867 as a result of experiences during the Danish War of 1864. The earlier model was made from grey cloth and the later one

Prussian General von Werder making a personal reconnaissance from the comfort of a carriage.

from dark blue cloth. Both models had six buttons and side pockets with flaps, and, like the French coat, the skirts could be folded back and fixed to the half belt at the back. The cuffs were plain. The collar of the 1832 model was a tall standing design closed by a hook and eye and had a red patch. The 1867 model was large and turned down, but in bad weather could be turned up to cover most of the face. It had a smaller red patch. In cold weather sentries were issued with a double thickness 'guard greatcoat', which was so cumbersome he needed his comrades help put it on.

Officers had an undress frock coat, termed a '*paletot*', which was double-breasted with two rows of six buttons and made from black material. It was piped red down the front, round the deep plain cuffs and on the rear skirts. The collar was all red, as was the chest lining which was revealed when the lapels were folded back. The coat reached mid-calf. For winter an overcoat was worn that extended below the knee. It was very dark grey, almost black, and double-breasted with a blue turn-down collar (green for *Jäger* officers). It had a half belt at the back which could be adjusted with two buttons. As the coat was not waterproof, a second coat of black rubberised material was authorised. This turned shiny when wet, so was not a popular item when French snipers were in the vicinity!

The most famous article of clothing used by the Prussians was the spiked *helmet*, the '*Pickelhaube*'. It was introduced in 1842, but whether it was invented by the Prussians or the Russians, who introduced a similar helmet at the same time, is not known. All Prussian infantry was issued with the helmet, but in 1854 the *Jägers* exchanged theirs for a leather shako. The helmet was made of two pieces of boiled and stiffened leather stitched together and with leather peaks at the front and rear. The front peak had a metal edging to hold the shape and another metal strip was added to the middle of the back of the helmet to cover the stitching. On top it had a four-leaf clover pattern piece of metal held by four studs with a metal spike rising from the middle. The helmet had a black leather chin strap covered in metal scales. These scales were attached to each side of the helmet by metal bosses. Inside the helmet was a leather liner which could be adjusted to fit the wearer's head with a leather drawstring. The former Prussian shako was adorned with a large metal heraldic eagle, which was now fixed to the new helmet with two metal screws. The original helmet was quite tall and subsequently heavy, and successive models were introduced to lighten it; the Model 1857 helmet was 42cm tall and the Model 1860 2cm lower. Another model authorised in 1867 had a smaller curved front peak and a circular base for the spike. It also dispensed with the metal rear strip. As each helmet had a useful life of ten years, models 1857, 1860 and 1867 were all worn during the 1870 campaign. The state cockade was made from a stamped metal disc worn under the right-hand chin scale boss; the regiments numbered 93–96 had theirs in the colours of the cap cockade. Other small states had a Prussian cockade on the right-hand side and a second cockade, in their state colours, on the left. Second-class soldiers had a plain grey cockade on the right-hand side.

Prussian types of helmet, top, the 1860 model with the spike fitted to a cruciform base, below, the Model 1867 with a rounded peak and no metal spine at the back.

Prussian infantry overrun a French battery of artillery.

For special occasions, reviews and ceremonial parades some regiments unscrewed and replaced the helmet spike with a metal tube holding a horsehair plume. The Foot Guards had a white plume for their first and second battalions and black for the 3rd (Fusilier) Battalion. The Grenadier Guards regiments and the 1st to the 12th regiments, with the title 'Grenadier' in their names, wore black plumes. Musicians and bandsmen in all units wore red plumes. Officers mostly wore the Model 1867 helmet as they had them made to order following the introduction of the regulations. The metal fittings were either silvered or gilded and the spike was higher than the soldier's models. The studs at the base of the spike were star shaped. Cockades were made from stiffened silk and the white was replaced with silver and the yellow with gold. The 1st Foot Guards had a special mitre cap, based on the Napoleonic Russian grenadier pattern, for parade wear. It had a brass front embossed with a star and crown and was worn by the 1st and 2nd Battalions, the 3rd (Fusilier) Battalion had a slightly shorter model, both secured by metal chin scale straps.

Jäger battalions had a black leather *shako*, a model introduced in 1860. It had a black leather chin strap and, at the top front, a large cockade which was made of wood covered with black and white cloth, or velvet and silver for officers. Officer's shakos were made from black felt with leather peaks and top. For ceremonial duties, the shako was fitted with a black horsehair plume (red for musicians).

The *belts and pack* straps introduced in 1847 replaced the cross belts worn since the reign of Frederick the Great. Several European armies were experimenting with better ways of carrying ammunition and the soldier's kit, and Prussia adopted the design of Captain Virchow. This was based on a leather waistbelt which supported one or two ammunition pouches and was connected to the pack by two shoulder straps. The straps terminated, at the front, in a metal clip which was hooked under the waistbelt, the other ends of the shoulder straps were sewn to the top of the back. Two small black leather straps were also fixed to the top of the pack, underneath the shoulder straps, which were buckled to the bottom of the pack to stop it bouncing around on the march. The waistbelt had a brass plate at the front with a white metal circle bearing the initials of the king, '*WR*', and the motto '*Gott mit uns*' ('God with us'). With the belts came a new pack of untreated cow hide with a light internal wooden frame, which was replaced in 1867 with a slightly smaller and lighter version without the wooden frame. It also had a large pouch on each side to carry packets of ammunition. Some older style packs were still carried during the war. Inside the pack was the soldier's drill trousers, underwear, shirt, spare boots or camp shoes, socks, field cap as well as material for cleaning man, uniform and weapons, and bags of 'iron rations', rice, salt and coffee. Personal items such as writing materials were held in any convenient place and on top of the pack was a roll of bandage. Fully loaded the pack and contents weighed 60 pounds (27kg).

Added to this each man carried a metal mess tin for cooking and eating which was strapped to the pack, either at the top or on the back. It was not unknown for some units to use 'liberated' French four-man mess tins. A single strap held the soldier's small haversack, used to carry food, but also for spare ammunition. It was made of grey linen and had a waterproof flap closed by two buttons. A water-bottle was only made an official issue in 1867, before that, soldiers bought their own or used captured Austrian wooden flasks. The Prussian model was made of glass covered in black leather with a cork

Prussian Foot Guard musician, with shoulder wings and full dress plume.

stopper and was carried on a black leather sling. It had not been universally issued by July 1870 and many men continued to carry privately purchased items or, after the start of the campaign, found the standard French issue superior. Junior NCOs carried similar equipment, whereas senior NCOs only carried the haversack and water-bottle. Officers were issued a small black leather pack with simple shoulder straps but tended to rely on their batman or company supply wagons for transporting it. Officers did carry a water-bottle, either issue or private, leather bags of similar size to the small haversack and sometimes telescope cases or field glasses or a revolver in a holster as they desired.

In addition to the load each soldier had to carry, to march and often to fight in, every man carried two small vital pieces of kit. When they received their pay, which was issued every ten days, after necessary deductions, any coins remaining were held in a small leather pouch hung round their neck. A card with a zinc plate displaying a soldier's regiment, company and army number was also worn around the neck.

As well as the regular pioneer companies attached to each army corps, every infantry regiment had its own pioneer detachment, carrying a selection of tools, axes, picks and shovels for minor duties. The tools were carried strapped to the left side of the pack.

Men in the infantry could be identified by company and battalion by the coloured *sword knot* which was tied around the frog of the short sword or the hilt of the sword bayonet in the fusiliers. It had a white strap with a 'crown', 'stalk' and 'head' and finished in a white tassel. The 1st Battalion had a white stalk, the 2nd a red stalk and the 3rd (Fusilier) Battalion a yellow stalk. The first companies in each battalion (the 1st, 5th and 9th) had a white crown and head, the second (2nd, 6th and 10th) a red crown and head, the third (3rd, 7th and 11th) a yellow crown and head, and the fourth (4th, 8th and 12th) a light blue crown and head. The *Jägers* had all green sword knots.

All infantrymen carried a *sidearm*, a short sword, although its use as a weapon was quite rare. However, it was very useful for chopping wood, or making a slight shelter to fire from and there was even an instruction to use it as a rifle rest by hammering it into the ground. It had a heavy steel blade and a brass cross-shaped guard and was carried from a frog from the waistbelt. There was no provision for a bayonet to be carried as it was invariably fixed to the barrel of the rifle. The fusilier regiments carried a similar shaped weapon, but this could be fixed to the rifle as a bayonet (fusilier rifles did not carry a fixed bayonet). The *Jäger* also carried a slightly different pattern sword bayonet. All scabbards were made of wood bound with blackened leather and had brass fittings. Sergeant-majors and officer candidates were not issued with rifles and carried a Model 1816 sword, which had an almost rapier-thin blade with a black hilt. This weapon was carried by company officers, while mounted officers carried a steel sabre with a guard, housed in a steel scabbard with cavalry slings. Some leeway was given to officers who could, with permission, carry a family-owned blade, which in at least one case dated back to the war with the first Napoleon. Swords were more of a display of rank and ceremonial item than a practical weapon, although a number of Prussian officers got hold of the French Model 1854 dragoon sabre complete with steel scabbard for their own personal use.

As regards *cold weather gear*, officers and soldiers were provided with a pair of grey cloth earmuffs which tied under the chin and a grey cloth hood worn under the field cap or helmet, which was large enough to cover the collar of the greatcoat. It had a slit either side for the helmet chin scales. Officers had a special hood that went over the cap or helmet and ended in a point halfway down the back. Officers and senior NCOs had white leather gloves, but in cold weather they and the rest of the infantry wore grey cloth mittens.

Rank

The lowest grade above private was lance-corporal, who wore a large button, decorated with a Prussian heraldic eagle, on either side of the collar. The corporal and the officer candidate had either silver- or gold-coloured braid (depending on the colour of the tunic buttons) round the top of the collar and round the cuffs. sergeants, deputy sergeant-majors and sergeant-majors had the same braid with a small version of the lance-corporal's button. the sergeant-major and the officer candidate had the officer's version of the cap and helmet cockade, and the officer's sword knot. Corporals and sergeants had a sword knot with a white strap with black lines and a knot of mixed white and black (white and green in the light infantry).

Officer grades were shown on the shoulder straps, which were of thin silver braid for company officers (2nd lieutenant, 1st lieutenant and captain) edged in silver/black/silver piping along three edges. It was backed by a piece of cloth in the same colour as the regimental facings. There was no decoration for 2nd lieutenant, one gilded 'pip' for a lieutenant and two 'pips' for a captain. Field officers (major, lieutenant-colonel and colonel) had thick twisted silver chord, no pip for a major, one gilded decoration for a lieutenant-colonel and two for a colonel. The most important indication of rank was the sash worn by all officers. It was made of a silver net-like material with two black stripes running along the length of the sash. It was worn around the waist and was buckled on the left side so that it hung down, ending in silver tassels with black material on the inside of the tassel. Officers doing the duty of adjutant wore the sash over the right shoulder. The sash was only worn with the tunic and frock coat. Officers also had a special sword knot with a strap similar in colour to the sash and all-silver knot.

Prussian Colours and Standards

The basic style of Prussian flags was a white silk sheet with details painted in oils, a black cross *pattée* with a central device of an eagle within a wreath and a crown and sovereign's monogram in each corner of the white sections. The sheets were about 5 feet (1.5 metres) square. Guard regiments had a plain white sheet with gold or silver decorations and the *Landwehr* regiments had the infantry standard in reverse – that is, a black sheet with a white cross *pattée*. Cavalry sheets were smaller, about 20 inches (51 centimetres) square of double thickness with an embroidered design and fringes around the edges.

Prussian Uniforms

The Palace Guard Company

The Palace Guard Company was a ceremonial guard at the royal palaces at Berlin, Potsdam and Charlottenburg. It consisted of five officers, seven NCOs and 62 men who were all rated as corporals. They had a blue tunic with a red collar and round cuffs, and a row of 14 white lace bars across the chest from the neck to the bottom of the skirts. Each bar terminated in a silver button and white fringes. White lace adorned the collar and cuffs, and the white shoulder straps had a gold crowned 'FR' monogram. White trousers were worn. For parade dress the Palace Guard wore a Foot Guards mitre cap, with silver front plate and chin scales, a red cloth back and white lace. For gala dress white breeches and stockings were worn. For undress they had a blue frock coat with a red collar with silver lace, and a single row of six silver buttons, red piping down the front. They also had an infantry helmet with a silver eagle plate and a guard star. For walking out a dark blue field cap with red band and piping and a black leather peak was worn.

Prussian senior NCO standard bearer.
(Author's collection)

The Infantry

Among the infantry the blue tunic was almost universal. Individual regiments and branches of service could be distinguished by the colour of the shoulder straps and the collar and cuffs. The Guards and Line infantry had poppy red collar and cuffs, the four regiments of Foot Guards had two white lace bars on either side of the collar and two white lace bars on each plain round cuff. The 1st Regiment had plain white shoulder straps; the 2nd, red; the 3rd, yellow; the 4th, light blue; and the Guard Fusiliers, yellow. Buttons were white metal (officer's silver) for the 1st Regiment and Guard Fusiliers, and yellow metal (officer's gilt) for the 2nd, 3rd and 4th. Officer's lace bars on collar and cuffs were in the button colour. The junior regiments of the Guards, the Guard Grenadiers, had yellow collar lace (gold for officer's) and red cuffs with blue cuff flaps with no lace. The 1st Regiment had white shoulder straps with a crowned letter 'A' in red, the 2nd red straps with a yellow crowned 'F', the 3rd yellow with a red crowned 'E' and the 4th light blue with a red crowned 'A'. The Guard's helmet badge had an eagle with spread wings in the colour of the tunic buttons with a silver 'Guard' star on its breast.

Each North German army corps had its own shoulder strap colour, some further distinguished by a piping round the cuff flaps.

Army Corps	Regiments	Shoulder straps	Cuff flap piping
I	1, 3, 4, 5, 33, 41 ,43, 44 and 45	White	White
II	2, 9, 14, 21, 34, 42, 49, 54 and 61	White	None
III	8, 12, 20, 24, 35, 48, 52, 60 and 64	Red	White
IV	26, 27, 31, 36, 66, 67, 71, 72, 93 and 96	Red	None
V	6, 7, 18, 19, 37, 46, 47, 58 and 59	Yellow	White
VI	10, 11, 22, 23, 38, 50, 51, 62 and 63	Yellow	None
VII	13, 15, 16, 17, 39, 53, 55, 56 and 57	Light blue	White
VIII	25, 28, 29, 30, 40, 65, 68, 69 and 70	Light blue	None
IX	75, 76, 84, 85 and 86	White	Yellow
X	73, 74, 77, 78, 79 and 91	White	Light blue
XI	32, 80, 81, 82, 83, 87, 88, 94 and 95	Red	Yellow

Prussian attack formation, skirmish line in front, followed by the company column with the battalion in the rear and artillery support. Note the mounted officers. (*Illustrirte Zeitung*)

However, as soon as the campaign opened operational pressures forced several regiments to change their army corps, but they retained their original colours. In addition, the regimental number was added to the shoulder straps, in red-on-white, yellow and light blue, and yellow-on-red straps. A few regiments replaced the number with a monogram showing a historical or state affiliation.

The Cavalry

The cuirassiers were considered heavy cavalry, the rest light. Each regiment consisted of a staff and five squadrons, except for the *Garde du Corps*, which had a staff and ten companies. The peacetime strength of a regiment was 25 officers, 713 NCOs and men, and 672 horses. In the field the regiment had four fully mobilised squadrons with 23 officers, 649 NCOs and men, four officials and 705 horses. The fifth squadron remained as the depot. It was not unusual to move troops around in forming the depot squadron: the best horses and men were transferred to the field squadrons and the worst horses and men sent to the fifth!

The Guards

The Guard Corps was commanded by Prince Augustus of Württemberg and consisted of two infantry divisions and a cavalry division. This comprised the *Garde du Corps* (Life Guards), the Cuirassiers of the Guard, three regiments of lancers, two regiments of dragoons and one regiment of hussars. Attached were the Guard Regiment of Field Artillery, pioneers and Train troops.

The Cuirassiers

As befitted their status as heavy cavalry the cuirassiers wore armour in the form of helmets and front and back plates. Each regiment had a name and a number in the Prussian order of battle. In addition, each regiment had coloured facings on the tunic (called a '*koller*') and white or yellow metal buttons. The *koller* was made of a woollen cloth, kersey, slightly yellowish white in colour and closed down the front with 14 or more hooks and eyes instead of buttons. Down either side of the front opening, round the collar and around the square-cut cuffs was a stripe of lace with three lines of white and two lines of the facing colour. The facing colour was also shown on the collar patches, cuffs piping on the shoulder straps and piping on the false pocket flaps as well as the rear seams of the *koller* and the backs of the sleeves. The *koller* of the troopers was lined with grey canvas, or with white wool or silk for officers. There were two buttons on each cuff, one on each shoulder to secure the shoulder straps and three on each false pocket flap. The unit colours were: *Garde du Corps*, red with white buttons; Guard Cuirassiers, cornflower blue with white buttons; 1st, black with yellow buttons; 2nd, deep red with white buttons; 3rd, sky blue with white buttons; 4th, red with white buttons; 5th, rose-red with yellow buttons; 6th, deep royal blue with yellow buttons; 7th, lemon yellow with white buttons; and 8th, light green with yellow buttons. The two Guard regiments had a single bar of white lace on the collar and two on the cuffs. Trousers were made of the same whitish kersey cloth, tucked into very high black leather boots that had soft tops that could be turned down.

The polished steel cuirassier helmet had a ridged square-shaped front peak and a 'lobster tail' curved neck guard, brass chin scales covering the leather strap. The Line regiments had the Prussian heraldic eagle plate also in brass. The exception was the 6th Regiment which had a tombac metal (a copper-zinc alloy) helmet with a nickel-silver plate. The two Guard regiments had a tombac metal helmet with a nickel-silver 'Guards' star on the front. The front and back plates of the cuirass were of iron, with the 6th and the Guards regiments having tombac. The cuirass had brass shoulder scales and a black leather belt, buckled at the front. Arms were a long straight sword, either a 'French' style with a brass three-bar hilt (these were copies of the French Napoleonic Year XI heavy cavalry sword or may even have been originals captured in 1815!), or a 'Russian' style with a two-bar hilt. A percussion pistol was issued, but not much used, except maybe when escorting prisoners. The sword had a knot the strap of which was made of red leather with a white fringe and a crown in the squadron colour, white for the first, red for the second, yellow for the third and light blue for the fourth.

For undress the two Guards regiments were issued with a dark blue tunic that could be worn by other regiments provided they paid for it themselves. The tunic buttoned down the front and had regimental lace on the collar and cuffs, which were in the facing colour, the 6th excepting of course by having poppy-red collar patches. It had white shoulder staps piped in the facing colour. In addition, the officers of the *Garde du Corps* had a gala tunic of bright red with blue collar and cuffs with two guard lace bars on the collar and two on each cuff. It had white piping on the collar, cuffs, down the front opening and on the false pocket flaps. Troopers had a white drill jacket and trousers for stable dress in the same style as the infantry. For duties on foot long dark grey trousers piped red were worn and some units still used the former dark-grey riding trousers with leather reinforcing and red piping.

The field cap had a white crown with a band and piping in the facing colour. The Prussian cockade was fixed in the centre of the band. Senior NCOs and officers added a small black leather peak to their caps. Every trooper carried a black leather pouch on a white leather shoulder belt. It held ten rounds for the pistol and a small bag for the percussion caps with a ramrod fitted under the lid. The lid had a round brass badge embossed with a Prussian eagle for the troopers (silver star for the Guards) and a gilt crowned monogram 'FWR' for officers. The officer's belt was of metallic lace in the button colour and piped in the facing colour. Like the infantry the cuirassiers had a grey greatcoat with collar patches in the facing colours. The officer's *paletot* had the facing colour on the collar, the inside of which was blue. The overcoat was in dark blue with collars in the regimental facings, apart from the 6th which was poppy red.

The Dragoons

The dragoons started their life in the Prussian Army in 1631 when a company of 200 men was formed. In 1870 they were still wearing what was essentially an infantry uniform, although training for fighting on foot was limited. The dragoons numbered two Guard regiments and 19 Line regiments (the 17th and 18th were Mecklenburg units, regarding which see below). The tunic was the infantry model in cornflower-blue cloth with regimental facings displayed on the collars, shoulder straps and round cuffs. Piping in the regimental colour down the front of the tunic and on the rear false pocket flaps. There were eight metal buttons down the front, two on each cuff, and one button on each shoulder and three at the back of the tunic on each of the false pockets.

Regimental colours were: 1st Guards, 2nd Guards, 1st, 5th and 13th, red; 2nd, 6th, 14th and 19th, black; 3rd, 7th and 15th, rose-red; 4th, primrose-yellow; 8th and 16th, yellow; 9th and 10th, white; 11th and 12th, crimson-red. The collars and cuffs of regiments 13–16, the newly raised regiments after the 1866 war, were white. Buttons were yellow metal for the 1st Guards, 1st, 2nd, 6th–9th, 11th, 13th and 14th, and the rest were white metal.

The dark-grey overalls with leather inserts and red piping (rose-red for the 3rd, 7th and 15th; crimson red for the 11th and 12th Regiments) were in the process of being changed to blue-black trousers, lined in black leather tucked into black riding boots. The 2nd Guards and the 8th, plus most of the officers of the other regiments wore the trousers; however, most of the troopers wore the overalls.

The helmet was the 1860 model with square-cut front peak and rear metal spine. Fittings were brass for those regiments with yellow metal buttons and white metal for those with pewter buttons. Chin scales were brass for all. The Prussian eagle on the helmet plate differed from the infantry model by having upswept wings and the claws grasping a sword and sceptre instead of an orb and sceptre. The field cap had a cornflower-blue crown and a band and piping in the facing colour. The NCO and officer's model had a small black leather peak.

A white waistbelt and pouch belt was worn by the troopers. The sabre was carried in a steel scabbard and had a steel basket hilt. Officers and NCOs of the 2nd Regiment carried a Napoleonic *chasseur* sabre taken from the French in 1815. Some troopers were armed with the Model 1850 percussion pistol which was attached to a strap hanging from the pouch belt; otherwise, the Dreyse carbine was carried, either attached to the saddle or the pouch belt.

The Lancers

After the fall of the first Napoleon and his army in 1815, many European countries raised their own regiments of lancers, those in Prussia, of course using the German word '*uhlan*'. In 1870 the Prussian Army comprised three regiments of Guard *uhlans* and 16 Line regiments. They were often brigaded with the cuirassiers and were regarded as heavy cavalry.

The lancer's tunic was called a '*ulanka*' and was a dark-blue double-breasted garment with collar, pointed cuffs and piping in the regimental colour. The piping went round the plastron shape, along the front and rear skirts and down the false pocket flaps and along the rear seams of the *ulanka* and the back of the sleeves. The front, with its plastron shape, had a button just below the shoulder and six buttons from mid-chest to waist on each side, three on each false pocket flap and two in the small of the back. There was a further button just below the point of each cuff as well as a small button on each shoulder to secure the epaulettes. These had the straps in metal, the colour of the buttons and a half-moon also in metal. The straps and pads were in coloured cloth. On the pads was a metal number of the regiment. The small retaining bridle on the shoulder was in the colour of the epaulette cloth. The Guards regiments had two bars of lace on the collar and one on each cuff in the button colour.

The facings colours were: red for the 1st and 2nd Guards, regiments 1–8; yellow for the 3rd Guards and regiments 11 and 15; light blue for the 12th and 16th; white for the 9th and 13th; and carmine for the 10th and 14th. Buttons were brass for the 2nd Guards, 1st–4th and 9th–12th, and white metal for the rest. The metal epaulettes were white metal for the 1st and 3rd Guards, 5th–8th and 15th, and brass for the rest. The cloth of the straps and pads was: white for the 1st Guards, 1st, 5th, 9th and 13th; red for the 2nd Guards, 2nd and 6th; yellow for the 3rd Guards, 3rd, 7th, 11th and 15th; light blue for 4th, 8th, 12th and 16th; and carmine for the 10th and 14th.

The trousers were, like the dragoons, in the process of being changed from overalls to trousers and boots. Most units continued to wear the grey overalls with leather reinforcement and red piping (carmine for regiments 10th and 14th).

A new model of the distinctive lancer headdress, the 'shapka', was introduced in 1867. The older model from 1844 had a black leather crown with a peak edged in brass and brass chin scales. The flared top finishing in a mortar board shape was black with a brass heraldic eagle plate similar to that worn on the infantry helmet and a large white and black cockade fixed to the front left edge. It had cords attached to the front right corner which fell down the back, tied round the neck and finishing in flounders and tassels hung from the top button of the plastron. The new cap, which was worn by most regiments, was lighter and lower and had the plate fixed to the skull. It was made of leather and painted black. The 1st and 3rd Guards had the Guard eagle plate with Guard star in white metal, the 2nd Guards a yellow metal eagle plate with white metal star. The lancers wore a blue cloth girdle edged in the facing colour. The field cap had a dark blue top with piping and a band in the facing colour. The pouch belt and waistbelt were as the dragoons, with the sword belt worn underneath the *ulanka*. They carried the dragoon sabre, a percussion pistol and a black-painted wooden lance about three metres long with a white leather strap. Officers had the same uniform, but with silver or gilded buttons and epaulettes and cap badges. For parade dress the *ulanka* had a facing colour plastron buttoned to the front and the shapka had a ribbed cloth covering the neck of the mortar board. The lance had a white-over-black pennon.

The Hussars

The Prussian Army had one Guards regiment and 16 Line regiments of hussars, still wearing vestiges of Napoleonic uniforms. The tunic issued to the hussars was called an '*attila*' a single-breasted garment that was closed by five rows of braid, buttoned with toggles and loops and the ends of the braid decorated with rosettes and Hungarian-style loops. The braid also appeared on the back seams and the rear skirts and around the collar and cuffs. Loops of braid were worn on the shoulders instead of cloth straps. The *attila* was coloured according to the regiment which also had either white or yellow braid and rosettes. The black sealskin fur cap had brass chin scales and a national cockade at the front. The cap had a leather binding on the bottom edge and a cloth bag falling on the left side.

Regiment	Atilla	Braid/rosettes	Cap bag	Officer's sabretache
Guard	Red	Yellow	Red	Red
1st	Black	White	Red	Red
2nd	Black	White	White	Black
3rd	Red	White	Red	Red
4th	Dark brown	Yellow	Yellow	Dark brown
5th	Deep red	White	Madder red	Black
6th	Dark green	Yellow	Red	Red
7th	Deep blue	Yellow	Red	Red
8th	Dark blue	White	Light blue	Dark blue
9th	Cornflower blue	Yellow	Crimson	Cornflower blue
10th	Dark green	Yellow	Madder red	Light blue
11th	Dark green	White	Red	Dark green
12th	Cornflower blue	White	White	Cornflower blue
13th	Cornflower blue	White	Red	Red
14th	Dark blue	White	Red	Red
15th	Dark blue	White	Yellow	Yellow
16th	Cornflower blue	White	Yellow	Yellow

The cap had a metal scroll badge in the braid colour and the Guard had a brass star while Regiments 1 and 2 had a nickel silver skull-and-crossbones. Regiment 7 had a brass crowned monogram, 'WR'. It was usual to hook the chin scales up behind the cockade when not in use. The officer's fur cap was slightly taller than the troopers and made from brown otter fur. The braiding on the officers *attila* was in silver or gold, in place of the white and yellow of the troops. In full dress the hussars had a sash of black wool with white knots, officers were silver with black silk. Officers also had a second *attila* with simplified braiding, a single, thin line around the collar and a single loop on the cuffs. The field cap was unusual in that each regiment had a different colour scheme, the top of the cap as the *attila* and the band in another colour with white or yellow piping. Officers and NCOs had a leather peak. A Prussian cockade was worn on the lower band, black with a white centre for the enlisted men and black metal with a silver centre for officers. Regiments 1 and 2 had a small silver 'Death's Head' badge on the upper part.

The same comments given for other branches of the cavalry apply to the hussar's legwear. Most still wore the overall trousers, with relatively few wearing the new tight trousers and boots. The latter extended almost up to the knee and had a strip of braid and a loop at the top. Arms were a light cavalry sabre carried in a steel scabbard suspended by black straps from the waistbelt, which was worn under the *attila*, together with a black leather sabretache which had a nickel silver or brass crowned 'FWR' monogram depending on the colour of the braid. Officers had a

Prussian hussar with field equipment.

sabretache in the colour shown in the table above with braid edging. The troopers of the Guard Hussars also wore the coloured sabretache, red with yellow braid. Hussars also carried the Dreyse carbine on a white shoulder belt. Pouches were as for the cavalry generally.

The Artillery

After the war of 1866 against the Austrians, the artillery was slightly modified, hence the model C64 became the C64/67, these were the 'light' 4-pounder guns, the 'heavy' batteries had the C64 6-pounder pieces. As well as the guns themselves, each battery had 6–8 ammunition wagons, three supply wagons, a field forge and a baggage wagon. Each light battery carried with it 922 shells, while a heavy battery carried nearly double that number. An artillery school had been established in 1867 to train gunners, even to the extent of practicing firing at moving targets. The artillery was charged with producing the army's ammunition for firearms and field and siege guns and it supervised a factory at Spandau near Berlin and a second in Silesia. The director of each factory was an army officer, but the workers were civilians.

The artillery wore the infantry uniform, but with a black collar and cuffs piped red. The spike on the helmet was replaced with a ball. The shoulder straps were red with the regiment number in yellow. The Guard artillery had two yellow lace bars on the collar and on the round cuffs. Foot artillery batteries had the infantry cuffs with blue cuff patches; the mounted batteries had round cuffs like the Guards. Foot batteries had the infantry trousers and boots, mounted men the dragoon overalls, although they were being replaced by tight trousers and boots. The mounted driver who rode the left-hand rear draught horse had a special leather chap on the right leg which incorporated an iron splint. This was to protect the rider's leg from the pole. Both the Model 1860 and the Model 1867 helmet were worn, brass plate for the Line batteries, tombak for the Guards. Foot batteries had infantry belts and straps in white leather and packs, which were often carried on the guns or limbers or in the battery baggage. They were armed with a modified infantry side arm, with a longer blade and a brass handle, worn in a leather scabbard. Mounted men carried an old model light sabre housed in a steel scabbard from white belts and a percussion pistol. Shoulder belt and pouch were as the dragoons. The field cap was dark blue with a black band, both with red piping.

The Pioneers

One pioneer battalion was attached to each army corps, a total of one Guards battalion and 11 Line battalions. Not part of the corps structure, but under the command of each of the armies formed in 1870, were three field telegraph and three field railway detachments. Further field railway detachments were mobilised as the armies advanced as well as seven telegraph detachments. Also raised were a pontoon train, with enough material to span a 125-metre gap (410 feet) and a light bridge train to build a 57-metre (187 feet) bridge. They also had a column carrying entrenching tools. As well as their technical duties the pioneers were trained to fight as infantry if the need arose. At full strength each pioneer battalion had 74 wagons and over 430 draught horses, plus 26 riding horses.

The uniform and distinctions of the pioneers resembled the artillery, blue tunics with black collars and (round) cuffs with white metal buttons. Red shoulder straps with the number of the battalion in yellow cloth were worn. The battalion of the Guard had two white lace bars on the collar and two on each cuff. Dark grey trousers and black boots were as in the infantry. The helmet was either the 1860 or 1867 model with white metal fittings and brass chin scales. The field cap was the same as that used by the artillery. There was also a black leather belt and pack straps with a single ammunition pouch worn at the right of the buckle. As with the infantry they had a short drill jacket as well as a double-breasted drill work coat with horn buttons; it was cut loose so that it could be worn over the drill jacket.

Arms were a short version of the Dreyse rifle without bayonet. However, the pioneers carried the Model 1865 knife which was about 60cm (2 feet) long, had a useful saw-tooth back and could be fitted to the muzzle of the rifle when required. The wagons carried the tools of their trade, including axes, picks, hatchets, shovels, saws and measuring tapes. Pickaxes were meant to be carried by the men and were issued with a leather case.

The telegraph detachments wore the same uniform with letter 'T' on the shoulder straps of the tunic and great coat with the number of their detachment. The railway detachments had a letter 'E' (for 'Eisenbahn', 'railway'). The telegraph troops were issued with a helmet and field cap, but the railway troops had only the field cap.

The Train

Like the French Train the Prussian version was responsible for delivering food, materials, ammunition and evacuating the wounded. During peacetime the Train was of little importance as troops resided in barracks and most of the items they needed were available locally. Upon mobilisation, with the troops on the move, all the army's requirements had to be brought from stores, magazines and producers to wherever the troops happened to be located. The 12 peacetime Train battalions (including a Guard Train battalion) were reorganised as a staff, five provision columns, one field bakery column, one horse depot, three stretcher bearer companies, three corps hospitals, three division hospitals and a depot battalion of two companies. The transport compliment of the five provision columns was 160 wagons and 825 horses.

The Train had the standard dark blue tunic with yellow metal buttons; the collar, round cuffs and piping were pale blue. The shoulder straps were pale blue with the number of the battalion in red. The Guard battalion had lace on the collar and on the cuffs. Overalls with leather protection for mounted men and infantry trousers and boots for those on foot were also worn. These had black belts and an infantry type sidearm as their only weapon. Mounted men had a white cavalry shoulder belt and pouch and a white waist belt with an old model steel-hilted light cavalry sabre worn in a steel scabbard. They also caried the percussion pistol. The Train troops wore a *Jäger*-style shako with a brass infantry eagle plate and a dark blue field cap with pale blue band and piping. The Guard battalion had a white metal star on their shakos. Officers had the same uniform, but they kept the leather helmet with brass plate or silver star for the Guards. Every unit, infantry, cavalry artillery and so on, had their own Train section who wore the uniforms of their parent unit, but with a field cap with a leather peak and chin strap.

The Medical Corps

Doctors formed a special place in the Prussian Army; they were not officers but received many of the privileges due an officer. The doctors served with their units in the field and were supplemented by medical professionals from the reserve or former *Landwehr* units. However, this was not enough to deal with the sheer numbers of the injured and volunteers were called for. Some 2,000 civilian doctors answered the call, with most serving in the rear areas or base hospitals, as did the mainly British and American volunteers. Medical students were taken on as assistants. Doctors were graded and wore shoulder staps as army officers. The British Ambulance Corps was raised to serve with the Prussian Army, but also cared for captured French wounded. The 'B' Division was commanded by Surgeon William Manley, a British officer who had served in the New Zealand Wars and been awarded the Victoria Cross for his bravery in trying to rescue the wounded during the action at Gate Pah. The Prussian Crown Prince recommended Manley for the Iron Cross Second Class for his services – the only Briton to receive both awards. The Ambulance Corps comprised 11 doctors, six NCOs and 21 men, plus eight ambulance wagons and 12 general service wagons. Its provisions, besides medical supplies, included 450kg (1,000lbs) of preserved meat, the same of biscuit, 110kg (250lbs) of preserved potatoes plus cocoa and sugar.

The Prussian doctors wore a blue tunic with gilt buttons and red piping. The collar and round cuffs had gold lace bars. Their epaulettes were the same as Prussian officers, lined with blue velvet and a gilt medical badge of the rod and entwined snake, the rod of Aesculapius. As doctors were not officers, they did not wear the officer's silk sash, but did carry a light sabre. Headwear was the leather helmet, but most medical staff are shown in the blue peaked field cap with red piping. Every regiment had its own medical orderlies, who wore a plain blue tunic with red piping on the collar, round cuffs and shoulder straps, and yellow metal buttons. Full dress infantry helmet with brass fittings was worn while for undress this was a field cap of dark blue with red piping. Orderlies carried a large pouch with first aid equipment, mainly bandages and a flask of something to revive the wounded! Every army corps had a stretcher bearer company with the blue tunic having a carmine collar, round cuffs, shoulder straps and piping, along with the corps number on the shoulder strap. The buttons were made of tin. The Guard company had white lace on the collar and cuffs. The field cap was worn in all orders of dress, dark blue crown with a carmine band and piping. Although medical personnel wore a red cross on a white armband, the idea of their non-combatant role was not yet fully accepted. Stretcher bearers were at first issued with a percussion pistol and later with a Dreyse carbine.

The Staff Guard

At the outbreak of the war a mixed force of staff guards was created. At the royal headquarters it consisted of an infantry officer and 220 men and a cavalry officer and 150 mounted men, all lance-corporals. Further guards were assigned to corps, division and brigade headquarters. Their uniform was a green tunic with a cornflower blue collar and cuffs, green cuff patches and red shoulder straps with the corps number in yellow, and brass buttons. The dark grey trousers had red piping with a broad cornflower blue stripe either side of the piping. The black leather helmet had brass fittings and chin strap. White belts and staps with infantry equipment were worn. The mounted men had a green tunic piped red, with a cornflower blue collar with a single bar of yellow lace, cornflower blue pointed cuffs with a single button. Their brass epaulettes had a red cloth backing. Cavalry riding trousers had leather inserts. They wore a steel cuirassier helmet with brass fittings.

The Courier Corps

This was a high-level courier corps with three officers and 73 men all ranked as sergeant-majors or officers and used for official business between royal headquarters, the army headquarters, the Foreign Ministry in Berlin and major embassies. The uniform consisted of a dark green tunic with red collar and round cuffs each decorated with two gold lace bars; gilt buttons and epaulettes with red cloth backing; dark grey trousers piped red; a black leather helmet with gilt eagle and a silver guard star and gilt chin scales. For parade dress a black falling plume was added in place of the spike. A light cavalry sabre was carried in a steel scabbard (a black waist belt and sword slings was worn beneath the tunic). The sword knot was silver with two black silk lines and a silver knot.

Officials

Administrative positions in the Prussian Army were filled by military officials, divided into 'military persons' and civil servants. The former were not actually officers but had some of the privileges, while the latter were civilians. Included in this class were 'apothecaries' (what we now call chemists) who assisted the doctors; paymasters who looked after pay books, distributing pay and keeping accounts; veterinaries, who were found in the cavalry, artillery and transport, and were NCOs who had graduated from the army's veterinary school; judges and clerks for the military courts. The intendants were of two types: the 'military' who were responsible for the direct supply of the troops; and the 'civilians' who looked after the garrisons, hospitals and magazines. There were also some organised clergymen of Lutheran and Calvinist faiths as well as Roman Catholics where the make-up of regiments warranted it. There were no official Jewish representatives, but services were held in the field on an ad hoc basis. The full dress for officials was based on the dark blue tunic with black or blue collars and round cuffs with red piping, but white for paymasters. The leather infantry helmet had white metal fittings, while the peaked field cap was blue with piping to match that of the tunic.

The Field Police

On the outbreak of the war, *Feldgendarmerie* units were raised from the Prussian state police force. They were used for general policing duties such as maintaining order in the areas around troop billets and garrisons, searching buildings, villages and so on for weapons, enemy soldiers, spies etc. preventing the looting of villages along the army's route of march, patrolling the battlefield, prevention of looting of the dead and wounded, support of requisitioning, serving with field courts martial, transport of prisoners, bringing prisoners to collecting points, the collecting and passing on of stragglers, keeping the roads free to the rear of advancing troops, protection of supply columns from looting and theft and traffic control at bridges. The police uniform was a dark green tunic, piped red, with pale green collar and round cuffs with yellow lace and corporal's rank lace round the collar and cuffs. Green shoulder straps were piped red. Trousers were the dark grey, piped red infantry trousers for foot troops and trousers tucked into riding boots for mounted units. Weaponry included a rifle and short sword for foot troops, while cavalry units had a straight sword. The infantry helmet had yellow metal fittings and an eagle with a silver guard star

The Field Post

The postal service in the field was a vital part of keeping up the morale of the army. It was staffed by men from the Prussian postal service (many of whom were retired soldiers) with each corps having a field post office with their own officials and wagons. It is said that after a battle, a wounded man would look for a member of the field post to relay news of his survival back home before seeking medical aid. It is estimated that the field post delivered 89 million letters and pieces of mail during the conflict. Pre-printed cards were issued to soldiers to fill in their details and add a short message. The field post also delivered letters and parcels from the homeland to troops in the field with small comforts, socks, scarves and sausages! The Prussian field postman wore a double-breasted tunic with a red collar and cuffs and brass buttons, and dark grey riding trousers. His field cap had a blue top piped red and a red band, with a cockade on the red band and a hunting horn badge (still the logo of the German postal service) on the upper part. He carried a large leather satchel over the left shoulder for mail and a cord in the German colours, black/white/red over the right shoulder from which hung a brass bugle so that he could announce his presence.

German Field Post and escort.

The *Landwehr* Infantry

By an order made in September 1867 all conscripts having served their seven years in the active army or reserve were posted to the *Landwehr*. This force had started life in 1813 as a citizen militia, but quickly ran foul of the higher military authorities as it was deemed too 'civilian' and democratic in outlook, with many of its officers not being members of the gentry. By 1870 it had been organised to the satisfaction of the authorities as a proper adjunct to the active army. Each regiment of the army was twinned with a *Landwehr* regiment taking the same name and number. Each regiment had two battalions except for the Foot Guards *Landwehr* regiments, which had three. Each battalion had a strength of four companies. The fusilier regiments numbered 33– 40 in the Prussian order of battle each had a single *Landwehr* battalion. The *Landwehr* uniform was the same as the active army regiments except that they wore a shako, similar the *Jägers*, in place of the helmet. On the front of the shako was a large oval metal plate, black with white edging and a white metal *Landwehr* cross in the centre (a *cross pattée* of a similar shape to the Iron Cross medal). The oval plate on the Guard shako had a brass star with the cross superimposed on it. Above the plate was a Prussian cockade, white with a black centre. The black leather chin strap was fitted with brass chin scales for parade dress. Officers had the regular helmet with the *Landwehr* cross on the breast of the eagle plate. However, there is evidence that some officers wore the shako painted a gloss black. The field cap was the same as the active army regiments with the addition of a small *Landwehr* cross superimposed on the cockade. Again, there is evidence that the *Landwehr* cross was placed above the cockade on the upper part of the cap. The first battalion of a *Landwehr* regiment wore white belts and straps and the second battalion, black.

Prussian Reserves bid farewell to their families.

The *Landwehr* and Reserve Cavalry

The *Landwehr* cavalry had been disbanded at the start of the war with 16 reserve cavalry regiments raised in their place. Two regiments were allocated to each of the Prussian Army corps. There were three reserve dragoon regiments, seven reserve lancer regiments and six reserve hussar regiments. The regiments had the same compliment as the regular regiments with four field squadrons, although some regiments had five or even six squadrons. The troops were meant to wear the uniforms of their respective branches of the cavalry with the addition of a white metal *Landwehr* cross on the headgear. There seems to be considerable variation in what exactly was worn, however. The 3rd Reserve Hussar Regiment had the uniform of the 2nd Hussars, but some men wore a felt and leather bound mirliton cap instead of the fur busby. This tall cap had previously been worn by the *Landwehr* cavalry and had brass chin scales with the number of the regiment in metal on the front and a large oval cockade, with a black centre on the right side, with a white *Landwehr* cross beneath it. The 4th and 7th Reserve Lancers were retitled the 1st and 2nd Reserve Heavy Cavalry Regiments in August, the 2nd taking the uniform of the 8th Cuirassiers, with light green facings on their *kollers*. Photographs of the reserve heavy cavalry show officers and men without the cuirass. Bismarck is often depicted in a heavy cavalry regiment's uniform, the 1st Reserve, which used the white *koller* with yellow facings of the 7th Cuirassiers. He also wears the blue undress frock coat with the field cap of a white crown and a yellow band. The reserve cavalry was used during the war as escorts for the many French prisoners sent back to Germany and for guarding the lines of communications.

Depot Battalions

Many cavalry regiments raised depot squadrons from new recruits and ex-*Landwehr* men. They were used to garrison fortresses in Germany and as guards for the large numbers of French prisoners of war. Their strength eventually rose to between four and six officers, 10–14 NCOs and over 225 troopers. In view of their duties, they were not mounted but would have worn the uniforms of their parent bodies, whether they were cuirassiers, dragoons, lancers or hussars.

Garrison Battalions

Those men of the reserves and the *Landwehr* who were not considered fit for active service in the infantry were formed into garrison battalions, as all able-bodied depot troops and *Landwehr* men had been sent to the field regiments fighting in France. They were commanded by reserve and recently retired officers and eventually comprised strengths of between 500 and 600 men. They were employed in guarding prisoners of war. They had no special uniform but wore the dress of the unit where they were originally mustered. They were armed with a variety of weapons, including converted rifles captured during the 1866 conflict.

Schools

Prussia maintained a number of schools specialising in various aspects of training. A gymnastic school in Berlin taught officers and NCOs the principles of physical education and bayonet fighting to be passed on

French captives escorted from the battlefield.

to the pupil's regiments. The riding school in Hanover taught potential riding masters for the mounted arms. Also, there existed a school in Berlin to train army doctors. The Potsdam infantry instructional battalion taught advanced infantry skills, including drill. As soon as war broke out it was disbanded. The marksmanship school was also closed for the duration of the war. The four NCOs schools were also closed at the start of the war but were reopened in October because of the losses among the ranks of corporals in the August battles.

The German Navy

Prussia had a small navy as far back as 1684 when its predecessor state, Brandenburg, established a trading post in West Africa. The colony was abandoned in 1720 and with it the German Navy. Brandenburg and after it, Prussia, had no need of a navy until the outbreak of the First Schleswig-Holstein War in 1848, when Prussia mobilised to help their fellow Germans and soon felt the need to re-invest in naval affairs. The Danes had a large and powerful fleet that dominated the North Sea and the Baltic. They could, and did, take the initiative and move troops by sea to strike at the Schleswig-Holsteiners wherever they chose. The Federal German government, set up by the revolutionary parliament, sitting in Frankfort, raised a small navy, under the energetic Admiral Brommy to challenge the Danes, and Prussia set about forming a naval force of its own to defend its coasts and coastal trade. Several vessels were bought from abroad and a home-grown ship building industry was begun. By the end of the conflict the Navy consisted of three sailing frigates, five steamers propelled by paddle wheels and a number of small gunboats for use on the Baltic Sea powered by both oars and sails. After the war interest in the Navy continued and in 1853 a Prussian Admiralty was set up and further sail and steam powered ships were purchased. The Prussian state had no natural harbours and, as an expedient, the government bought some land from the Grand Duke of Oldenburg and started to build a naval base which later became known as 'Wilhelmshaven'.

In the 1860s the European naval powers began to replace their 'wooden walls' with a new design built with iron plates fitted to their hulls. This was a very expensive process and Prussia had spent its entire military budget on raising new regiments for the army. When the Second Schleswig-Holstein War broke out in 1864, Prussia's wooden ships stayed in the shelter of their ports and in the end an Austrian squadron sailed into the North Sea from the Mediterranean to engage the Danes with something like parity.

After the victory, on land, against Austria and her allies in 1866, the Prussian government acquired a North Sea and Baltic coastline to defend with little prospect of being able to do so. Bismarck had envisaged that a war against France might be an inevitability and France, under Napoleon III, had developed a powerful naval armament, second only to the British Royal Navy. The North German Confederation was given the task of building a navy strong enough, not necessarily to defeat the French, but sufficient to make the French think twice about forcing a decision at sea. The plan called for 16 ironclads and 20 un-armoured screw-driven frigates, plus smaller ships. However, lack of funds again hindered the programme and in the first three years after the end of the war, just three armoured frigates were bought from British and French shipyards. By 1870 the Navy consisted of five ironclads and nine steam-powered frigates, plus some sailing ships and a number of steam-powered gunboats.

As well as Wilhelmshaven on the North Sea, the new port developed at Kiel, in the former Danish territory of Holstein, served ships in the Baltic. Naval policy, common to all European powers, was to station ships around the world to protect merchants and trade in case of need. As a result, when war broke out with France some German ships were far from their home ports.

The main strength of the fleet was composed of the five armoured battle ships, three armoured frigates and two other ironclads. The two armoured frigates, SMS *Kronprinz* and SMS *Friedrich Carl*, were both built in 1867 in British and French yards for Prussia. They were about 7,000 tons and carried 16 21cm guns. They were similar to the ships of other European navies. There were two smaller ironclads (iron plates fitted to wooden hulls): the SMS *Prinz Adalbert* (1,560 tons) and SMS *Arminius* (1,829 tons). While the latter was designed as a monitor, influenced by the American Civil War, SMS *Prinz Adalbert* was built for the Confederate American Navy as a ram ironclad (*Widderschiff*). Further smaller vessels took little part in the war, apart from the frigate *Augusta* which was sent out into the Atlantic as a commerce raider, actually capturing three French transports before making for Vigo in Spain to avoid a French squadron and spending the rest of the war there. The only other conflict involved the gunboat *Meteor*, which found itself outside the harbour of Havana facing the French gunboat *Bouvet*. After a battle both sides drew off, the German having inflicted considerable damage on the French ship but taking some hits itself. She sought shelter in Havana where she was forced to stay until the end of hostilities.

SMS *Arminius* was armed with four 21cm guns and a 35cm torpedo tube (a new weapon the Germans had yet to test). It was not before 1880 when the weapon was recognized for the potential it had, when *Kapitanleutnant* Tirpitz, later Grand Admiral of the German Navy, commanded the torpedo test cruiser SMS *Blucher*. SMS *Prinz Adalbert* was armed with one 21cm and two 17cm guns. It was known as the 'Lame Prince', as due to bad wood used in its construction it tended to leak. The flagship, in 1870, was the armoured frigate SMS *Konig Wilhelm*. Originally built as the *Turkestan*, later *Fatih*, for the Ottoman Navy, the ship was sold to Prussia because the Turks could not afford to pay for her, and the British Navy did not want it. SMS *Konig Wilhelm* was the most powerful ship on the seas at that time. It displaced 10,761 tons and carried 18 24cm and five 21cm guns.

Add to these ships a number of so-called 'flush decked corvettes' (sloops) called '*Glattdeckskorvetten*', including SMS *Nymphe, Medusa, Augusta* and *Victoria*, of 2,272 tons and armed with eight 24-pounder and six 12-pounder guns, as well as the lightly armoured corvettes ('*Gedeckte Korvette*') SMS *Arcona, Elisabeth, Gazelle, Vineta* and *Hertha*. These last were of 2,300 tons weight with an armament of 17 15cm guns. A number of gunboats were used as escorts. These were divided into the gunboats first class, including SMS *Camaeleon, Comet, Cyclop, Meteor, Delphin, Blitz, Basilisk* and *Drache*. They displaced 422 tons and were armed with one 24-pounder (15cm) and two 12-pounder (12cm) guns. There were also the second-class gunboats SMS *Jäger, Crocodill, Hay, Scorpion, Fuchs, Sperber, Hyne, Habicht, Pfeil, Natter, Schwalbe, Salamander, Wespe, Tiger* and *Wolf*. These 283-ton small ships had the same armament as the larger gunboats. There were also two avisos (fast courier ships): SMS *Preuischer Adler* and *Grille*. The first one displaced 1,430 tons and was armed with four 24-pounder guns and the second, which was also classed as the Prussian royal yacht, displaced 491 tons and was armed with two 12-pounder guns. These smaller ships were built in German yards.

During the war only one new ship was added to the complement: SMS *Falke*, an aviso of 1,230 tons with an armament of two 12cm guns. Originally constructed in a Scottish yard for the American Confederate Navy, it was sold to a Dutch company as the Confederate government could not find the cash to pay for her. In August 1870 it was bought from the Dutch by a 'Mr John Smith of London' who turned out to be *Korvettenkapitan* Graf von Waldersee who brought it to the Prussian port of Emden where it was later transferred to Wilhelmshaven to be fitted out as a warship. However, it was badly damaged on its first operation by being accidently rammed by SMS *Arminius*. As the only available dock was occupied, the damage had to be repaired piecemeal. The ship was finally repaired in 1871 but did not re-enter service until 1875.

Other German ships were the old sailing ship of the line SMS (formerly the Royal Navy's HMS) *Renown* and the frigates SMS *Gefion, Niobe* and *Thetis*. These ships were used as training ships as they were hopelessly outdated by modern armoured ships. They were either employed as harbour guards or for training.

The ships remained in their bases apart from the SMS *Hertha* and *Medusa* which were both in East Asia; SMS *Meteor* in the West Indies; and SMS *Arcona* at large in the Atlantic.

Personnel for the navy were conscripted as in the Army, but from the North German Confederation provinces which bordered the sea. The term of service was three years whereupon one was passed to the reserve for four years. Naval recruits were called back for two weeks each year for training. As in the army, after the reserve the man was mustered into the naval version of the *Landwehr*, the *Seewehr*, where he stayed on the roll for five years. As with any country with a coastline and a merchant marine, experienced seamen did join the navy as volunteers. A proportion of naval officers were taken from the Merchant Navy, and more were admitted from volunteers from titled families.

The common fault with this system was that none, or almost none, had any wartime experience and no large-scale exercises had ever been undertaken. To compound the problem, Prussia being a state with a powerful army for its size (or as some would say, since the time of Frederick the Great, an army with a state!) had no naval hierarchy, the minister responsible for the Navy in the Prussian cabinet was War Minister General von Roon! The head of the Navy was Prince Adalbert of Prussia, a distant cousin of King Wilhelm. The real commander was Rear-Admiral Jackmann, who had begun his career as a cabin boy in 1839, later transferred to the Navy as a cadet and worked his way up to be an officer and eventually as the most senior naval officer after Prince Adalbert. The Prussian Admiralty was responsible for all naval armaments, technical developments and ship and shore construction. Even then it was under the leadership of an army major.

The manpower of the navy consisted of an officer corps of four admirals and 150 other officers and 100 officer cadets, a seaman's division of 75 warrant officers, 321 petty officers and 2,150 seamen, plus 330 ships boys (in effect seamen or sailor cadets), and a technical division including tradesmen, medical assistants, and machine specialists and stokers totalling 779 men. With the outbreak of the war the seaman's division stood at 3,923 (on mobilisation to 5,824) and the technical division to 918 (1,411) men. These numbers were still not sufficient to man all the vessels of the Navy.

In 1857 a naval infantry battalion and an artillery section were formed. The naval infantrymen were mainly intended for coastal defence, although a small number served on board the larger ships, including 100 officers and men on the flagship, the *Konig Wilhelm*. The battalion had a wartime strength of 1,254 officers and men. Enough reservists arrived at the depots to form a reserve battalion; however, it was disbanded at the end of the war. In peacetime the artillery section was responsible for making ammunition, but on the outbreak of the war it manned the guns of all the shore establishments. It had a strength of six companies with a total compliment of 1,149 men.

In full dress officers wore a low crowned cocked hat with a gold loop on the right side securing a Prussian black/white/black cockade; a dark blue double-breasted coatee with gilt buttons, with three further buttons on each round cuff; gold epaulettes with a silver anchor and gold bullion fringes. The lapels were worn buttoned back, faced white with gold lace edging. There was also gold lace to the collar and one to four gold lace stripes to denote rank on the cuffs below the three buttons. The blue trousers had broad gold stripes down the outside seams. Service dress was a dark blue frock coat worn open to show a dark blue or white waistcoat and white shirt with a black bow tie, and dark blue trousers. Although there was no gold rank badges on the cuffs, officers did have a cord shoulder strap similar to the hussars. Officers carried a sword with a lion's head pommel with one red and one green eye. The sword knot was as the army and the scabbard was black leather with gilt fittings. Officer cadets and midshipmen did not wear a sword but a short dirk with a white handle carried in a brass scabbard, with an officer's sword knot. Midshipmen also wore a silver and black lace cord on the collar held with a small button to denote rank. All officers wore a blue peaked cap with a gold band with a Prussian cockade on the front. Warrant officers wore the officer's uniform, but without rank badges, instead sporting a crowned gold fouled anchor badge on either side of the collar. Their cap had a narrow gold band.

Prussian naval officer and sailors. Pictured are a sailor wearing infantry equipment, an officer, and a senior NCO.
(*Illustrirte Zeitung*)

Lower ranks wore dark blue double-breasted jacket and trousers with yellow metal buttons. The jacket was worn open to show a blue or white shirt and a black tie. The shirt had a large medium-blue collar edged with three white stripes. In full dress the headgear was a black lacquered leather hat, the brim turned up all the way round; in service dress a dark blue round cap with a black ribbon hanging loose at the back. On the front of the ribbon the words, '*Königliche Marine*' appeared in yellow. Rank was shown on the upper left arm by a gold fouled anchor. For action on shore, sailors wore infantry belts and pouches and were armed with the Dreyse rifle, without the fixed bayonet.

Prussian ships, those which were powered by steam, were painted black with yellow masts. Where they had paddlewheels, the paddle boxes were white. The *Prince Adalbert* showed a red band just above the waterline. The sailing fleet had a white band along the level of the gunports. All North German Confederation vessels flew the 'war flag', a white rectangle with a straight-edged black cross, the so-called 'Scandinavian cross' like the Danish and Swedish emblems with the upright arm set closer to the pole, edged with a thin black line. In the centre of the cross there was a white disk with a black Prussian eagle. In the upper section next to the pole there was a German tricolour of, from the top, black/white/red and with a *cross pattée* in the centre. Various pennants were flown, usually white with a black *cross pattée* emblem to denote senior officer's commands.

The Prussian Navy Ironclad *Prinz Adalbert*.

During the war the changes in circumstances allowed the use of sailors on land. *Korvettenkapitan Freiherr* von Reibnitz led a detachment against French gunboats on the Rhine during the siege of Strasburg. A detachment was also sent to the mouth of the Seine to block the passage of shipping bringing supplies to Paris. On the Loire, German sailors under *Leutnant zur See* Jeschke captured six French gunboats. A token company of about 100 men was also sent to Paris as part of the besiegers, which caused quite a stir when they were reviewed by the King of Prussia. The press made wild guesses as to the meaning of sending sailors to Paris: Was the army running out of soldiers, one surmised?

4

North German Confederation: Prussia's Allies

After 1866 the states of North Germany who had fought for Prussia and those states who had been defeated signed conventions with Prussia putting their armed forces under Prussian control. There were changes in organisation, weapons and uniform to make them fit in with the army and corps system of the Prussian Army.

Brunswick

Brunswick contributed an infantry regiment of three battalions, a regiment of hussars and a single battery of artillery of six 6-pounder guns to the North German Confederation Army. The 3rd Battalion was named the 'Life Battalion' because of its previous history. Also for historical reasons, the rank of corporal was termed '*Oberjäger*'. Brunswick never actually signed a convention with Prussia in 1867, as did other small German states (due to the intransigence of its reigning duke, Wilhelm), but its government agreed to recognise the minutes of the negotiations. The Brunswick troops formed Infantry Regiment number 92 of the German establishment and Hussar Regiment number 17. The artillery battery formed the 4th Battery of the 2nd Foot Battalion of Field Artillery Regiment number 10.

As a direct result of not signing the convention in 1867 the infantry battalions retained essential elements of the uniforms worn during the Battle of Waterloo. The tunic was called a '*Polrock*' (literally, 'a Polish coat') and was made of black woollen material with cornflower blue collar and shoulder straps and pointed Polish cuffs. The front of the tunic was closed by ten black glass buttons each with a strip of black frogging ending in a fringed rosette. Two further buttons were situated at the back of the tunic, which was decorated with more black frogging ending in a knot design. The buttons on the shoulder straps were in metal and painted black, apart from the company number. The shoulder straps had a crowned 'W' in black cord. Black trousers piped in cornflower blue down the outside seams and black boots were also worn. Headgear was a shako, similar in shape to Austrian and French styles with a felt body and leather top, lower band, peak and chin strap. The 1st and 2nd Battalions wore a white metal eight-pointed star plate, the 3rd Battalion (the former Life Battalion) a white metal skull and crossbones plate over a metal battle honour scroll with the letters 'PENINSULA' embossed on it. A small black falling horsehair plume was fitted above the state cockade, yellow with a blue centre, for parade dress, but was frequently worn in the field. Black leather belts, straps and pouches were as those in Prussia. The Prussian-style field cap had a black crown with cornflower blue piping and a cornflower blue lower band with the state cockade in the centre. NCOs had British-style rank chevrons, in flat silver braid on a cornflower blue cloth backing on the upper right arm. Corporals had two chevrons, sergeants three, and sergeant-majors four. Sergeants also had a waist sash of cornflower blue with two white stripes ending in blue/white cords and tassels. The cords were tucked under the sash so that the tassels hung down at the front. In full dress NCOs of the 3rd Battalion wore green leather gloves, while NCOs of the 1st and 2nd Battalions had white gloves. The greatcoat was black with white metal buttons and a cornflower blue collar patch and the shoulder straps from the tunic. The infantry carried the improved Model 1862 Dreyse rifle which came with a fixed spike bayonet. All soldiers carried a grey or white bread bag that hung from a white cloth strap and the Prussian-style glass, leather-covered water-bottle.

Officers also had a black *Polrock*, but with five toggles in place of buttons and rows of hussar braid on the chest. The collar and cuffs were cornflower blue with black braid in a Hungarian knot design above the cuffs. Company officers (up to captain) wore a band of gold lace and field officers (major upwards) a wide band of gold lace on collar and cuffs almost covering the blue material. Their trousers were the same as the men's, but boots were taller and varied between black and brown, obviously private purchases. There were silver plates on the shako. In the field and in undress officers had a small soft kepi, similar to an Austrian cap, in black cloth with a black leather peak and chin strap, with a small button and loop at the front and a metal cockade, gilt with a blue centre. Gloves were the same as those for the NCOs. The 1st and 2nd Battalions carried a straight sword in a steel scabbard, the 3rd Battalion a slightly curved blade in a black leather scabbard. Field officers wore the sash of silver net with two cornflower blue stripes on campaign. Shoulder straps had a gilt crown and a 'W' monogram. Officers wore a black leather belt supporting the sword and were hung about with the usual impedimenta, field glasses in a case and privately purchased pistol in a holster.

The hussar regiment had an all-black uniform with five rows of yellow hussar braid on the chest. There was also yellow braid down the front of the *attila*, round the hem, top and bottom of the collar, along the false pockets below the waist and decorating the seams at the back. Toggles were of yellow metal. The black riding trousers had red piping. The hussar busby was black sealskin with a red bag falling to the left side with yellow cap lines and carried a yellow metal banderol embossed with the battle honours 'PENINSULA-SICILIEN-WATERLOO'. The busby had yellow metal chin scales and had a cockade that was yellow with a cornflower blue centre and a white over cornflower blue plume for parade dress. The barrel sash was cornflower blue with white barrels. The other ranks sabretache was suspended from red leather straps; it had a brown leather back, while the front was red and decorated with yellow and blue edging and a yellow crown and 'W.' monogram. The greatcoat was the regular Prussian long cavalry coat with red collar patches and shoulder straps with brass buttons. For undress troopers had a field cap, black with yellow piping on the headband and the crown, and NCOs had the piping in gold. Arms consisted of a Prussian light cavalry sabre carried in a steel scabbard and a Dreyse carbine carried on a black sling, to which was also attached a plain black pouch. The waist-length stable jacket was all black apart from yellow piping around the collar and a small yellow braid Hungarian knot above the cuffs. The black *shabraque* had pointed rear corners, yellow braid edging, yellow crown and 'W' in the rear corner.

Officers had a bearskin busby with silver mixed with blue silk cap lines. The field cap was the same as the one worn by officers of infantry. The *attila* had gold cord braid. An undress *attila* was black with black braid, buttons and rosettes. The officer's *paletot* was black. The pouch was red leather decorated with silver at the top and sides and hung from a red leather belt covered with gold braid. The officer's sash was silver interwoven with light blue silk threads. The sabretache was hung on similar belts and resembled the trooper's item with the addition of heavy gold and silver embroidery. Officers carried an old pattern cavalry sabre with a gilt basket hilt. The finely decorated sabretaches of both troopers and officers had a red leather cover in the field.

The artillerymen had a black *polrock* with black collar and cuffs edged in yellow braid. The collar had two strips of yellow braid ending in simple knots. Shoulder straps were black with yellow cord crown and 'W'. They carried the infantry shako with a brass star over crossed cannon barrels at the front with a cockade and black falling plume. The field cap was black with yellow piping. Trousers were black piped red with mounted men having leather protection to the inside of the leg. Officers wore the same uniform, but with gold cords replacing the yellow. They also had the peaked field cap and gilt shako plate.

Hesse-Darmstadt

After the war of 1866, this central German Grand Duchy was forced to sign an agreement with Prussia, putting its troops under their control. They formed the 25th Division of the North German Confederation Army, part of the 9th Corps with two infantry brigades, the 49th and 50th and the 25th Cavalry Brigade. They retained their organisation, numbering and uniforms until 1871 when they were incorporated into the Prussian system as the 115th to 118th Infantry Regiments and 23rd and 24th Dragoons. Each of the four regiments had two battalions with a total of eight companies, four in each battalion. When mobilised, each regiment formed a replacement battalion. The *Landwehr* consisted of four regiments bearing the same numbers as the regular regiments, but they were only ever at cadre strength. There were also two battalions of *Jägers*, each with four field companies. The cavalry consisted of two regiments styled 'light horse', but armed and equipped as dragoons, each with four field squadrons of 138 men each and one depot squadron. The artillery had two (heavy) batteries of 6-pounders, three batteries of foot artillery (light) and one horse battery with 4-pounders, all with six guns each. The reserve artillery had one each of heavy, light and horse batteries. There was a Train (supply) and a pioneer company. The divisional administration included a field intendancy, a field war chest (all German troops received regular pay on campaign!), field provisions section (including the bakery section), senior medical staff, six field hospitals, hospital staff, a field post section, auditors and two divisional chaplains (besides those attached to regimental and battalion staffs).

The Hessian infantry had a dark blue tunic, adopted in 1849, closed by eight buttons, with red shoulder straps, piping down the front and on the rear skirts and false pocket flaps and around the 'Polish' (pointed) cuffs. They were distinguished by the colour of the collar, red for the 1st, white 2nd, bright blue 3rd and yellow 4th. All regiments had two white lace bars on either side of the collar. Buttons were white metal, one on the point of each cuff, two at each cuff flap piping one on each collar lace bars, three on each rear pocket flap and one on each shoulder strap. Dark grey trousers piped red and black boots were worn. The greatcoat was double-breasted in dark grey with white metal buttons and a collar patch in the regimental colour. All belts and straps were of black leather, and the belt buckle was brass embossed with the Grand Ducal crown. The Hessian ammunition pouches were stitched directly on to the waistbelt rather than hanging below it on straps. Arms were a Dreyse needle-gun Model 1862 and short sword. Attached to each sword was a knot identifying the company, straps were white with tassels of red for the first four companies, and white for numbers 5–8. The crown above the tassel were in the sequence, red (companies 1 and 5), white (companies 2 and 6), light blue (companies 3 and 7) and yellow (companies 4 and 8). The helmet introduced in 1868 had a few small differences from the Prussian model. It had yellow metal fittings with the plate of the Hessian lion within a wreath of laurel and oak leaves. Under the right chin scale boss was a cockade of white/red/white. The spike was fluted, and the helmet did not have the '*pearlring*' decoration at the base of the spike. Officers wore a similar uniform with silver buttons and gilt helmet fittings. In the field officers wore a *paletot*, tailored about the waist with a half belt at the back, which was double-breasted with a regimental colour collar patch. The dark blue field cap was piped in red round the lower band and the crown and had a state cockade at the front. The peak was of black leather, and it had an adjustable chin strap. The field cap was worn by all ranks from general to private.

The *Jäger* battalions had the same style uniforms as the infantry, with green collars and a red patch for the 1st Battalion and a white patch for the 2nd and only one lace bar and button. On each shoulder there was a green padded wing. Instead of the helmet they wore a felt shako with a leather crown and base, peak and chin strap, which was similar to the Austrian headgear of the period. On the front there was a plate as on the helmet and a white/red/white painted metal cockade, with silver/red/silver for officers. *Jägers* carried a small woollen plume, half green with a coloured top half in the company colour, red, white, light blue and yellow for the 1st to 4th. NCOs had a green plume with a 2cm-wide red band in the middle, officers an all-green plume, but held in a gilt 'tulip'. The troops carried the Dreyse M65 *Jäger* rifle with a sword bayonet attached to which was a white sword knot with green fringes with the crown in the company colour as worn on the shako plume. In the field the plume was often removed, and the shako covered in a black oilskin. Officers had a silver sash with three red lines and with knots and tassels. However, this was only worn in parade and gala dress, as it too easily marked out an officer in the field. They wore instead a waist sash without fringes, resembling a lancer waistbelt. Senior and staff officers continued to wear the dress sash, the staff officers carrying it over the right shoulder.

The two cavalry regiments had dark green tunics with red piping, the 1st Regiment with a red collar and the 2nd with white. Each had a black collar patch, almost completely covered by a bar of white lace. Scale white metal shoulder staps with red lining were worn and tunic buttons were of white metal. The uniform included dark grey cavalry overalls with red piping, but the decorations was almost covered with leather panels. The black leather pouch belt had a brass crowned initial 'L' on the pouch flap, and a waistbelt with a brass buckle. The helmet was of the infantry pattern with a black horsehair plume for parade dress. The cavalry field cap was dark green with red piping, black leather peak and chin strap. The cavalry greatcoat was long, covering the legs when mounted, with a standing collar with red patches for the 1st Regiment and white for the 2nd. For extra protection a short cape could be worn over the shoulders. The *shabraque* was dark green with rounded corners and wide white edging with a central black line and a white crown in each rear corner, silver for officers. Arms were a sabre with a steel hilt and either the old pattern Hessian percussion pistol or the Dreyse M57 carbine. The sword knot had a black strap with crown and tassels in red for the 1st squadron, white for the 2nd, light blue for the 3rd, yellow for the 4th and green for the 5th. Officers had silver buttons, lace and epaulettes, a silver pouch belt edged red with two red lines and a black leather pouch belt cover with silver studs. The pouch was black with a silver crowned initial 'L' within oak and laurel leaf branches. In field dress officers had a *paletot*, similar to the infantry, with regimental colour tabs on the collar. Epaulettes were not worn on the *paletot*. The waist sash was the same as that of the infantry.

The artillery wore the infantry uniform with black collars piped red, with the helmet carrying a spike instead of the ball of the Prussian artillery. Infantry trousers and boots or riding trousers, black belts and straps were worn. All gun carriages and wagons were painted grey with black metalwork. The pioneer company uniform had a crimson collar, shoulder straps and piping. The Train company had a blue collar, with a single lace bar and blue shoulder straps piped red and round cuffs with two buttons. Riding trousers had leather inserts. They were issued a shako like the *Jägers*, worn in a waterproof cover, but the officers used the helmet.

Other small administrative sections of the army had their own uniform. The tunics had a plain collar, without lace and 'Swedish' cuffs (round cuffs with two buttons on them; see the Prussian Foot Guard uniforms). The field ambulance section had madder red collar and piping with white metal buttons, officers with silver buttons and shoulder straps and dark grey trousers piped red. A black helmet with gilt fittings or a field cap with madder red piping were worn. The field bakery section had the uniform of the Train with grey lace collar bars and infantry trousers. Extra regimental functions such as paymasters had yellow collars and piping and yellow shoulder straps edged silver, yellow piping down the outside seam of the trousers. Auditors (that is, those keeping control of the regimental spending) had a light blue collar and piping, shoulder staps with silver lace. Intendancy (commissariat) officers wore light red collar and piping, silver shoulder straps. The *Gendarmerie* (militarised police) had a green infantry tunic with pink collar and piping, two white lace collar bars and a silver aiguilette crossing the left breast. Their shoulder straps were silver on a red backing ending in a large trefoil design. They wore cavalry riding trousers, and their saddle sheepskin cover had a pink edging. Either the infantry helmet or a green field cap with pink piping was worn.

Mecklenburg

The two related north German states, Mecklenburg-Schwerin and Mecklenburg-Strelitz, lay between the Baltic Sea and their large neighbour, Prussia. The larger of the two, Schwerin, was ruled by Grand Duke Friedrich Franz II who was related to the Prussian royal house through his mother, Princess Alexandrine, a sister of the Prussian king (and later German emperor) Wilhelm I. By 1870 the Grand Duke was a general in the Prussian Army, having taken part in the Second Schleswig-Holstein War (1864) and the Austro-Prussian War (1866). After signing the convention with Prussia in 1867 the two states fielded 6,680 men, 5,630 from Schwerin and 1,050 from Strelitz. The reorganised forces were added to the North German Army and numbered in the Prussian line as Grenadier Regiment number 89, the Fusilier Regiment number 90, *Jäger* Battalion number 14, Dragoon Regiments numbers 17 and 18 and the III Foot unit of Field Artillery Regiment number 9. Together they formed the 34th Infantry Brigade and part of the 17th Cavalry Brigade of the 17th Infantry Division of the 9th Army Corps.

The former Strelitz contingent became the 2nd Battalion of Grenadier Regiment 89. The old Guard Grenadiers of Schwerin formed the 1st Battalion. The peace strength of a battalion was 18 officers, 53 NCOs, 17 signallers (drummers), 444 privates plus 16 non-combatant workers (tailors, shoemakers), four medical orderlies, a paymaster and a gunsmith. At full strength each regiment consisted of 49 officers, five doctors, three paymasters, 230 NCOs, 51 signallers, 2,672 men, 66 Train soldiers, 12 medical orderlies and three gunsmiths, plus 116 horses for officer's mounts and the company's wagons. In the dragoons, the 2nd to 5th squadrons formed the field regiments, the 1st the depot. They fielded 23 officers, two doctors, a paymaster, three veterinary officers, 61 NCOs, three trumpeters and 571 troopers (17th Regiment) or 528 (18th Regiment).

The 17th Division was originally kept in northern Germany to counter any threat from a French landing or incursion from Denmark. As no invasion occurred, at the end of August the whole division was dispatched by rail to France and formed part of the Army to the west of Paris operating against the French Army of the Loire.

The infantry uniforms, while following Prussian styles, retained several distinctive features of their historical dress. The former guard grenadiers wore a dark blue single-breasted tunic closed with eight white metal buttons, two on each of the false pocket flaps at the rear; it had red cuffs with blue cuff flaps each with three white lace bars with white metal buttons and red collar, piped blue, with two white lace bars. White shoulder straps had a red crowned 'FF' cypher. The 3rd Battalion was similarly dressed. The 2nd Battalion had yellow metal buttons with yellow lace bars in place of the white, and red shoulder straps with a yellow crowned 'FW' Grand Ducal cypher. (The Grand Duke of Strelitz was Frederick Wilhelm.) The lace on the officer's uniform was embroidered with silver thread.

The 90th Regiment had a similar uniform with white metal buttons, but without the lace bars, and red cuff flaps piped yellow, white shoulder straps with the number of the regiment in red. The dark grey greatcoat had blue shoulder straps piped in white with the regimental number also in white. Both regiments had the Prussian dark grey trousers piped in red. All belts and straps and pouches were of black leather, and the brass belt buckle had a silver star bearing the Mecklenburg coat of arms. The helmet was the Prussian Model 1867 with a brass 12-pointed sunburst plate with the Mecklenburg coat of arms in the centre in white metal. The spike was fluted and terminated in a small ball. For parade dress the spike was removed and replaced with a holder containing a black horsehair plume. The state cockade of blue/yellow/red was worn under the right chin scale boss.

The *Jäger* battalion had the infantry uniform, but with the collar, cuffs and cuff flaps and shoulder straps in a fairly bright green, all piped red. The battalion number appeared in red on the shoulder straps. Headgear was the Prussian *Jäger* shako with the Mecklenburg helmet plate with the Mecklenburg cockade of red and blue quartered with yellow edging. Officers had a grey greatcoat with a dark blue collar. In full dress officers had silver epaulettes on red cloth backing secured with silver bridles with red threads. The gold sash had blue interwoven thread round the upper part and a similar red thread round the lower part. The fringes were mixed gold, red and blue. Officers of the 2nd Battalion of the 89th had gold bridles and gold epaulette crescents.

The infantry regiments had the Dreyse Model 1862 and the *Jäger* battalion the shorter Dreyse Model 1865. All troops were issued a bread-bag of blue cloth and a water-bottle covered in black leather carried on black straps.

The two dragoon regiments had mid-blue tunics with yellow metal buttons, red collars, shoulder straps and piping. The 17th had red cuffs, the 18th blue with red piping. Both regiments had two yellow lace bars on their collars and cuffs, and dark blue-grey riding trousers with leather inserts and black boots. The long grey cavalry greatcoats were single-breasted with yellow metal buttons, cornflower blue shoulder straps with red piping. The helmet was the infantry model, with a black horsehair plume for parade dress. Instead of a saddle cloth, a white sheepskin cover with red cloth edging was used. Troopers carried a sabre with a brass guard and a Dreyse carbine, NCOs a percussion pistol.

The artillery batteries wore a dark blue tunic with white metal buttons (yellow for the Strelitz battery), black collar with piping round the top and bottom edges, black cuffs and blue cuff flaps piped red and red shoulder straps. The Prussian style helmet had a plate the same as the infantry.

Saxony

After the war of 1866, the Saxon troops were incorporated into the North German Confederation Army, but on the understanding that they would form a separate army corps. Saxony also retained its own war ministry and the Royal Saxon Corps, numbered XII, had its own general staff. The chief of the Saxon Army during the 1866 war, Crown Prince Albert, who had shown considerable tactical skill, became the corps commander. It comprised two infantry divisions, the 23rd and 24th, and a cavalry division. The regiments retained their Saxon numbers but were also numbered in the Prussian establishment. The Saxon 1st Grenadier Regiment became the 100th Regiment; 2nd Grenadiers, the 101st; the 3rd Regiment, the 102nd ;4th, the 103rd; the 5th, the 104th; the 6th, the 105th; 7th, the 106th and the 8th, the 107th. The Saxon Schutzen (Fusilier) Regiment became the 108th, the 1st *Jäger* Battalion became the 12th in the Prussian list and the 2nd *Jäger*, the 13th. The 1st and 2nd Saxon Uhlan Regiments were numbered the 17th and 18th in the Prussian system. The Guard and 1st, 2nd and 3rd Cavalry Regiments retained their numbering, although they were the equivalent of dragoons. The corps also included a battalion of pioneers, a battalion of Train troops and a field artillery regiment of 96 guns. A fortress artillery regiment also existed. The Saxon Field Artillery Regiment number 12 was organised with four foot artillery battalions with a mix of 6-pounder and 4-pounder guns and a horse artillery battalion with 4-pounder guns. The newly supplied Krupp guns were fitted to the existing Saxon iron carriages. The carriages were painted light grey, and the guns blackened. The medical personnel manned the four base hospitals in Saxony.

From 1867 a *Landwehr* organisation was put in hand, but only enough men to form four battalions were raised. They were mobilised in August 1870 and sent to newly occupied Lorraine to guard lines of communications.

Saxony marched out to war in 1870 in new uniforms, based on Prussian models. The basic tunic was dark blue closed by eight yellow metal buttons, collar and square-cut round cuffs in red, the red piping extended down the front of the tunic and all around the hem and along the skirt flaps. Shoulder straps were in blue with rounded ends, rather than the pointed ends of the Prussian model, with red piping all the way round the strap and the regimental number (from the Prussian order of battle) in yellow, or a royal cypher for those regiments who had a royal colonel-in-chief (the 100th, 101st, 104th and 106th). There were two buttons at the rear seam of each cuff and two buttons on each skirt flap. The 100th Grenadiers had round cuffs with two white lace bars, which also appeared on the collar. The new woollen tunics were lined in the body with grey canvas and the tails with thinner black material. Trousers were the Prussian model of dark grey piped red and were tucked into short boots. Helmets were black leather with brass fittings, the plate was a brass eight-pointed sunburst with a silver-crowned Saxon coat of arms in the centre. The Saxon cockade under the right chin scale boss was a metal disc painted green/white/green. The infantry had a dark blue field cap with a red band and red piping round the crown, which was fitted with a narrow black leather peak and a chin strap. The Saxon cockade of green with a white centre was fixed to the red band. NCOs and men had the company number on the front of the crown above the cockade. Black leather pouches, belts and straps were worn; however, the shoulder belts were of a different design to the Prussian one, with narrow straps looped from shoulders to a metal hook on the waistbelt between the pouch straps. On the right hip hung a white bread-bag on a white strap and a metal water-bottle. The greatcoat had red collar patches with the tunic shoulder straps.

Saxon troops, infantryman, infantryman with pioneer tools, 'Reiter Regiment', artillery in the background.

Saxon Infantry Regiment drummer boy.

The Schutzen Regiment and the two *Jäger* battalions had a very dark green tunic with black collar and cuffs, red piping on the bottom edge of the collar, round the cuffs, down the front of the tunic, around the skirts and on the skirt flaps. The green rounded shoulder straps had red piping all the way round with the battalion number in red for the *Jägers* and a red hunting horn device with the regimental number ('108') for the Schutzen. The greatcoat had black patches on the collar and the tunic shoulder straps were worn on it. A low felt shako with leather top, peak and chin strap was worn, and the cap plate was the same as the infantry for the men of Regiment 108, but the metals were reversed, silver sunburst and gold coat of arms for the *Jäger*. The shako had a short black falling horsehair plume fitted to its top centre above the plate and tied up on the left side. In the field the shako was covered with a black oilskin. Other equipment was the same as for the infantry. The Saxon infantry carried the Dreyse Model 1862, the Schutzen Regiment the Model 1860 fusilier rifle and the *Jäger* battalions the Model 1865 rifle. The Saxon short sword was slightly larger than the Prussian model with a heavier blade.

Officers wore the same uniform as the men, but of finer quality material. In full dress gilt epaulettes without fringes were worn, but these were worn with fringes in ceremonial dress. Buttons were of gilt and there were gilt and silver helmet fittings. The waist sash was silver with two green stripes, tied at the left side and ending in mixed silver and green fringes. A frock coat, similar to the Prussian *paletot*, very dark grey, double-breasted, with two rows of gilt buttons was worn. It was tailored at the waist and had a small belt at the back. The turn-down collar was blue on the outside and red on the inside. The body of the coat was lined with red material. Officers were armed with a sabre carried in a steel scabbard, with the knot of silver with green edging. The belt was worn under the tunic and was red leather with gold decoration.

The four cavalry regiments adopted the tunic of the Prussian cuirassiers, in cornflower blue instead of white and with white piping, including the rear seams of the sleeves and the seams and false pocket flaps at the back of the garment. Collar and square-cut cuffs were in the regimental colours, white for the Guard regiment, bright red for the 1st, dark crimson for the 2nd and black for the 3rd. The piping and facing colours went round the collar, down the front of the tunic and round the cuffs. The front of the tunic was closed by concealed hooks and eyes. There were two brass buttons on the cuffs and two on each false pocket on the rear skirts. Brass fringeless epaulettes completed the tunic. Several different types of trousers were authorised, coloured cornflower blue with white piping, as well as riding breeches with leather reinforcement and tight-fitting riding trousers and high boots, though it is doubtful whether any of the last mentioned ever made it to the troopers. The helmet was unique to the Saxon cavalry and was a development of an earlier model. The Model 1867 was black leather with a rounded crown, and front and back peaks edged in brass, with two brass strips either side of the chin scale bosses. It had a black leather comb bound all round with brass with a black woollen crest as well as a state cockade worn under the right-hand side chin scale fixing. The plate was as for the infantry, brass sunburst with silver coat of arms. The Guard Regiment had a deep gold colour sunburst made from tombac, a mixture of copper and zinc. A white pouch belt with a plain black pouch was worn and the white sword belt was beneath the tunic. The greatcoat had a large vent at the back and pale blue shoulder straps piped white with a royal monogram for the Guards and a yellow number for the other three. All of them had a collar patch in the facing colour. A black sheepskin saddle cover was worn by all regiments. The field cap was cornflower blue piped white with the band in the facing colour. A sabre with a steel basket hilt was carried in a steel scabbard. There was a brass basket hilt for the Guards. Firearms were a Dreyse carbine for troopers and a percussion pistol for NCOs and cavalrymen carrying pioneer tools (each squadron had a few men detailed as 'cavalry pioneers', an innovation introduced into the Austrian dragoons some years before). Officers had a decorated pouch with gold and silver fittings on the cover, worn on a white bandolier which had a gilded Royal Saxon coat of arms. Gilded scale epaulettes and gold-plated fittings to the helmet, which also had the comb in gilt, completed the officer uniform. The horses of the Guard Regiment were always brown.

The two lancer regiments wore uniforms in the Prussian style, but the basic colour was a medium blue grey with a deep purple-red collar and cuffs piped white. Buttons and epaulettes were of brass. The 1st Regiment had two white lace bars on the collar and one bar on the pointed cuff which had a single button and the 2nd had yellow lace bars. The girdles were the same for both regiments, blue with two red stripes. Riding trousers were blue with a broad dark red stripe on the outside edge. Arms included a sabre, a Prussian percussion pistol and a lance with a white over green pennon. The pouch belt was white with a loop to which was fixed the pistol ramrod. The shapka was the black Prussian model with the Saxon helmet plate on the front and a Saxon white and green cockade fitted to the left front edge. It had brass chin scales and edging to the peak. The white woollen cap lines (green and white for NCOs) were tied round the neck and the tassels under the left epaulette. For full dress the upper part of the cap was covered in a coloured ribbed cloth, white for the 1st Regiment and dark red for the 2nd, both edged with white braid. The field cap was white for both regiments with a blue cap band for the 1st and dark red for the 2nd. The uniform for officers had the following distinctions: gilt buttons, epaulettes and shapka fittings, silver, and green silk cap lines. The top of the square cap was covered in regimental colour cloth, the edges trimmed with gold braid. They had the same pouches and pouch belts as cavalry officers. Trousers had a white piping down the outside seams with a dark red stripe on either side.

Artillery uniform tunics were green with red collar and round cuffs and piping and brass buttons. As with the infantry the red piping extended round the tunic skirts. Trousers were dark grey piped red, and mounted gunners had leather reinforced riding trousers. Shoulder straps were green edged red with a red embroidered '12' (the number of the corps in the Prussian Army order of battle). Mounted men had brass shoulder scales and epaulettes. The helmet was the Prussian ball-topped model with the Saxon plate and cockade. The field cap was dark green with a red band and piping. The foot gunners were armed with a short sword and mounted men with sabres and pistols. The greatcoat had a red collar patch and green shoulder piped red. Officers wore a sash and a pouch and pouch belt, the pouch bearing a silver coat of arms. The officer's greatcoat had a dark green collar, lined with red material on the inside and with red piping. The pioneers were part of the artillery regiment and wore the artillery uniform, but with white metal buttons. The helmet had white metal fittings, apart from the chin scales which were brass. The red shoulder straps had a red cloth emblem of a crossed pick and shovel over the number '12'. The Train troops wore a mid-blue tunic with black collar and cuffs piped red and brass buttons. They wore dark grey trousers and boots for foot troops and blue riding trousers for mounted men. Mounted troops also had brass cavalry epaulettes. Headgear was the Model 1862 felt shako, which had a leather top and peak, with a brass plate above which was fitted a blue pompon. It was often worn with an oilskin cover. The field cap was blue with a black band and red piping. The infantry greatcoat had black collar patches and blue shoulder straps piped red. The officer's coat had a blue collar lined with black and with red piping. The sash and pouch and belt were as the artillery. Saxon Field Post riders are depicted with a single-breasted tunic with red collar and cuffs and a blue cummerbund.

5

South Germany

Baden

Baden had been a reluctant member of Austria's allies in the South German Army in 1866 and was keen to make an agreement with Prussia. A convention signed in August 1866 effectively put Baden's troops under the control of the Prussian General Staff. Baden officers were sent for training to Prussian regiments and Prussian officers were installed in the Baden military organisation.

The Baden Army was made up of six infantry regiments each of three battalions with a peacetime establishment of 540 men per battalion, making a total of 9,700 men. The ten battalions of the field division had 10,600 men. The cavalry had three regiments of dragoons each of five squadrons, with a peacetime strength of each regiment 576 men. In time of war each regiment had four squadrons with 636 men. The artillery had one field regiment of nine batteries plus a Train (transport) division and five companies of the Fortress Artillery Battalion. The total peacetime compliment was 1,890 men. The pioneers had two companies with 250 men. The Train troops had 148 men. The Baden *Landwehr* was at cadre strength only, with ten battalions each of 136 men.

For field service the Baden Division was made up of ten battalions, 12 squadrons, nine batteries, for a total 16,000 men, 5,800 horses and 54 guns. The depot troops consisted of three battalions, three squadrons and one battery, making a total of 4,000 men. In addition, the garrison troops (guarding fortresses, and so on) had eight battalions, one squadron and five fortress batteries for a total of 9,600 men.

The Baden infantry uniform closely followed the Prussian model, with slight differences. The 1st (Life) Grenadiers wore a similar style to the Prussian 1st Foot Guards with white lace on the collar and round cuffs, white shoulder straps with a red embroidered crown and yellow metal buttons. The Model 1867 helmet had yellow metal fittings with the Prussian eagle being replaced by the Baden griffon (a mythical creature with the body of a lion with an eagle's head and wings), and the state arms. This helmet plate was the same for the whole army. There is evidence that some men wore the older style helmet, which had a higher crown, a square-cut front visor and a fluted spike rising from a cruciform support. Shoulder straps were white for the 2nd Regiment, red for the 3rd, yellow for the 4th, light blue for the 5th and green for the 6th. The 2nd Regiment had a red 'WR' monogram and crown, the 3rd the number in yellow and the other regiments had the number in red. Prussian equipment was standard issue and all regiments had black straps and belts. The haversack, worn on a black sling over the left shoulder, was of cowhide with the hair left on. Cockades on the helmet and field cap were in the Baden colours of yellow/red/yellow. Officers carried a sabre in a steel scabbard on red leather slings edged silver. The sash was silver with one red and one yellow seam. The sword knot was silver decorated with red and yellow. Baden bought Prussian Model 1862 needle-guns which equipped two regiments, while the rest had a Dreyse needle-gun copy made by the firm of Sauer & Spangenberg in Suhl, which was known as the 'Model 1867'.

Three dragoon regiments made up the Baden cavalry who wore Prussian-style uniforms with red facings and piping for the 1st (Life) Regiment, yellow for the 2nd and black facings with red piping for the 3rd. Buttons and helmet fittings of white metal. Overall trousers with leather reinforcement were worn. As well as sabres, either needle carbines or muzzle-loading pistols were carried.

Artillerymen had Prussian-style uniforms with a yellow grenade embroidered on the shoulder straps and black leather belts. Gun carriages and wagons were painted a browny/green-grey with metalwork in black.

One of a several designs for a 'volley gun' similar to the Bavarian 'Feldl' gun.

The Baden colours were of white silk with a large gold crowned 'L' for the reigning Grand Duke Ludwig on the obverse and the Baden arms on the reverse.

Württemberg

The south German kingdom of Württemberg retained many of its traditions from before 1866 but adhered to its treaty obligations with Prussia. Its eight infantry regiments each had two battalions and it disposed a further three *Jäger* battalions. A battalion had a peacetime establishment of 480 men and a wartime strength of 1,070 men. The field army consisted of 15 battalions with 16,000 men. There were four regiments of cavalry of four squadrons each and a small squadron (50 men) of *Feldjäger* (militarised police). The peacetime strength of a squadron was 496 increased to 676 in time of war. Only three regiments were employed in the field army. The artillery had a regiment with nine batteries, a division of fortress artillery with four batteries and two Train divisions. In peacetime there were 1,600 men, while in wartime the nine batteries had 1,900 men. There were also two pioneer companies and a Train column of 1,300 men. The *Landwehr* had just four battalions.

For service in the field the Württemberg Division had 15 battalions, 13 squadrons and nine batteries – in all 22,000 men and 54 guns. Remaining in the depots were 6,500 men and in garrison four battalions, one squadron and four fortress batteries, making a total of 6,000 men.

All branches of the service wore a dark blue double-breasted tunic with, for the infantry, a red collar, shoulder straps, padded wings and piping down the front of the tunic, around the hem of the skirts and round the plain blue cuffs. There were two rows of six white metal buttons, with two further buttons on the rear skirts. The company number was shown in blue on the shoulder straps. The regimental distinction was indicated by a small, coloured tab on each side of the collar. The Queen Olga Regiment (the 1st) wore white; 2nd, black; 3rd, orange; 4th, green; 5th, light blue; 6th, blue; 7th, deep red and 8th, yellow. Dark grey trousers with red piping were worn with black boots. For parade dress the infantry wore a low shako of blue cloth, but with a very wide red band, fully reaching halfway up the shako with a white metal plate showing the regimental number and the state arms. The shako had a black leather peak and chin strap and a red and black cockade. In field dress, a round soft cap was worn that was dark blue with red piping and a small cockade.

The belts and straps were black leather, with a single large ammunition pouch that could be moved round the belt as convenient. The haversack/bread-bag was of brown cowhide of the Baden pattern. Water-bottles were of the glass Prussian type. The dark grey greatcoat was worn strapped round all four sides of the backpack.

Officer's tunics were similar to those of the men, but without the shoulder straps and wings. They wore black caps with silver piping and black/red/silver cockades. The sash was crimson worked through with black seams, and the tassels were looped under and hung down at the front. Unlike the other German states rank was denoted by stars on the collar tabs as in the Austrian Army. The ranks of lieutenant to captain had one to three stars in the button colour, and major to colonel had gold or silver braid on the collar with one to three stars in the opposite colour to the braid. NCOs wore one to three stars in the button colour. In August 1870 officers were ordered to use Prussian shoulder boards to denote their rank, but the change took place rather slowly and they continued to wear the collar stars.

Jägers wore the same tunic as the infantry, but all red distinctions were replaced with green, including along the trouser seams. They also wore a marksman's award of green plaited cords looped across the chest.

Cavalry wore a similar tunic to the infantry, but with a blue collar piped red. Regimental collar patches were: 1st, light blue; 2nd, yellow; 3rd, red; and 4th, white. The tunic had yellow metal buttons. The cavalry wore the Prussian dragoon helmet with brass fittings and the Württemberg coat of arms on the front. Legwear was either grey breeches with a red seam tucked into black riding boots, or the older style leather reinforced overalls. All cavalrymen were armed with a sabre and a percussion pistol. Sword knots were white with tassels in the squadron colour: 1st, red; 2nd, yellow; 3rd, green; and 4th, black. Gold braid pouch belts and sword slings were also worn.

The artillery had a tunic with a black collar piped in red and a field cap with red piping. The tunic had white metal buttons, with silver for officers. Mounted artillerymen had overalls, whereas officers had breeches and boots. Gun carriages were painted greeny-grey. The pioneers had the artillery uniform with brass buttons, gilt for officers.

The small unit of *Feldjägers* wore the tunic, but with light blue cuffs and collar patches and yellow metal buttons. They had brass fringeless epaulettes and a yellow woollen aiguilette, gold cord for officers, from the right shoulder. Dark blue trousers with a broad light blue stripe with a red piping down the seam were also worn. Since the corps was raised in 1817, the headgear was a black bearskin with brass chin scales.

Officers in most orders of dress wore white gloves and for parade dress, the pioneers, artillery and *Jägers* wore a black falling plume on their shakos, as did the 1st, 2nd and 3rd Cavalry Regiments, with the 4th wearing white.

The greatcoat was dark grey with two rows of buttons to match the tunic, with red or light green piping around the turn-down collar, the cuffs and the half belt at the back. The officer's coat had no shoulder straps but had further piping on the front opening and side pocket flaps. As in the Austrian service it was traditional to wear it open to show the rank badges and the crimson sash.

The colours of the Württemberg regiments were a deep red with the cypher 'W' in gold (for the king, Wilhelm) on the obverse and the state coat of the arms on the reverse.

Bavaria

This south German kingdom of Bavaria had a long history of independence, and its origins can be traced back to late Roman times. In 1742 one of its rulers was elected to the throne of the German Empire. After Austria and Prussia, it was the third largest of the German states. In 1866 Bavaria joined the allies against Prussia and suffered as a consequence. Bismarck let the Bavarians off lightly, although they had to join his South German Confederation and conclude a military alliance with Prussia (then part of the North German Confederation). By 1870 the Bavarian Army had 16 infantry regiments each of three battalions and ten battalions of *Jägers*. With four companies, each battalion had a peacetime strength of 380 men which was increased to 1,012 in time of war. In round numbers the infantry had a peacetime strength of 22,000 men and a wartime strength of nearly 59,000 men.

The cavalry was comprised of ten regiments, two of cuirassiers, six of light dragoons and two of lancers, each of five squadrons. When mobilised, one squadron became the depot squadron. In peacetime the regiment had 690 men, but in the four squadrons of the wartime establishment, it had 583 men. Of the 7,000 cavalrymen, 5,800 took the field.

The artillery had four regiments each with eight field batteries, one siege, four fortress batteries and a Train squadron. Of the 32 field batteries there were four of horse artillery. All batteries had six guns. The 1st and 4th regiments had four 4-pounder and four 6-pounder batteries, while the 2nd and 3rd had six 6-pounder foot batteries and two 4-pounder horse artillery batteries. During the war a battery of four 'volley guns' was added to the 1st Regiment. These were four-barrelled, manually operated guns, similar to the French *Mitrailleuses*, but mounted on light wheeled carriages. They were designed by Johann Feldl and made at Augsburg in 1867–1868. They soon developed problems in action because of the barrels jamming but did manage to fire with only one of the four barrels functioning. The war strength of the artillery was 7,000 men. There was a regiment of engineers with six field companies, four of fortress engineers and a Train division, for a total of 1,400 men. There were also four Train companies with 3,000 men. The *Landwehr* had 32 battalions kept as cadres with 64 men in each of the four companies.

On a war footing the army consisted of 50 infantry battalions, 40 squadrons of cavalry and 32 artillery batteries, for a total of 69,000 men, 15,000 horses and 192 guns. Those remaining in the depots consisted of 16 battalions of infantry, ten companies of *Jägers*, ten squadrons of cavalry, eight batteries of artillery, two companies of pioneers and the garrison troops with eight regular battalions, 16 *Landwehr* battalions, 16 batteries of fortress artillery and four companies of pioneers – in all 23,000 men.

The Bavarian Palace Guard troop was a ceremonial unit, whose members were drawn from soldiers who displayed excellent character and conduct. The commander of the troop had the title *Generalkapitän*. The Palace Guard numbered five officers, eight NCOs and 100 men. They were armed with a straight sword and a glaive-style polearm in full ceremonial dress. In full dress they carried a carbine, a pouch belt and a carbine sling. The uniform was a blue tunic with black velvet collar and cuffs edged with thick silver lace. The 13 silver buttons extended from the neck to the skirts each decorated with broad silver boutonnieres, as were the two buttons on each cuff and the three buttons on the false pocket flaps at the rear. The silver lace covered the whole chest at the neck, narrowing at the waist and broadened again on the front skirts. Shoulder straps were of blue cloth with broad silver lace. White leather riding trousers and thigh-high black leather riding boots were also worn. In ceremonial dress the boots were grey suede, in the same style as the riding boots. Also for ceremonial dress a supra-vest was worn over the tunic, which was of white cloth with pleats at the lower edge, silver embroidered blue wings and the front panel was embroidered with the star of the Bavarian House Order of St Hubert in gold and silver bullion thread with a red velvet centre with the embroidered motto of the order '*IN TRAU VAST*' ['FIRM IN FIDELITY']. All belts were blue with wide silver lace and gauntlet gloves were worn. The helmet was silver with a gilt plate of the Bavarian coat of arms, edging to the peak and a standing golden lion on top. In full dress the supra-vest was not worn and the lion on the helmet replaced by a spike with a white horsehair falling plume and the gloves were worn without the gauntlet cuffs. The calf-length greatcoat was white with a blue turn-down collar. For walking out dress the tunic dispensed with the heavy silver lace, and plain blue trousers and the peaked field cap with a silver crown badge were worn.

There has been much discussion regarding the blue uniforms worn by the Bavarian Army. Illustrations show all shades of mid- to light blue; however, photographs of surviving examples are close to the cornflower blue of the Prussian Dragoons. The vegetable dyes used at the time were not as stable as the later chemical dyes and a report of the victory parade of Bavarian troops in Munich in 1871 speaks of the infantry tunics fading towards purple! The infantry and *Jäger* battalions wore the blue tunic closed by a single row of eight metal buttons, with a further two on the round cuffs and three on each false pocket flap at the rear. The tunic had red piping down the front and on the rear false pockets, and red padded shoulder wings. The regiments could be distinguished by the facing colours and button material.

Life Regiment	Red collar/cuffs*	White buttons	M1868 helmet	Podewils rifle
1st Regiment	Deep red	Yellow buttons	?	Podewils rifle
2nd Regiment	Black**	Yellow buttons	?	Podewils rifle
3rd Regiment	Red	Yellow buttons	?	Podewils rifle
4th Regiment	Yellow	White buttons	M1868 helmet	Podewils rifle
5th Regiment	Rose red	White buttons	M1845 helmet	Podewils rifle
6th Regiment	Red	White buttons	M1845 helmet	Podewils rifle
7th Regiment	Rose red	Yellow buttons	M1845 helmet	Podewils rifle
8th Regiment	Yellow	Yellow buttons	?	Podewils rifle
9th Regiment	Crimson	Yellow buttons	M1845 helmet	Podewils rifle
10th Regiment	Crimson	White buttons	M1868 helmet	Podewils rifle
11th Regiment	Black**	White buttons	?	Podewils rifle
12th Regiment	Orange	White buttons	?	Werder rifle
13th Regiment	Dark green**	White buttons	?	Werder rifle
14th Regiment	Dark green**	Yellow buttons	M1868 helmet	Podewils rifle
15th Regiment	Orange	Yellow buttons	M1845 helmet	Podewils rifle

*White button lace on the cuffs.
**Red piping to collar and cuffs.

The Podewils rifle the Army used was a compromise weapon and suffered accordingly. It was originally introduced into the Bavarian Army in 1858 as a muzzle-loading percussion rifle manufactured by August Francotte of Liege, Belgium. After the 1866 war it was converted to breech-loading using a system designed by Lindner. The 'Podewils-Lindner-Braunmuhl system' rifle fired a paper-covered bullet and powder charge which was detonated by a hammer striking a percussion cap. The calibre was 13.9mm. The gun was slow to load as the percussion cap had to be fitted on the nipple before the bullet could be inserted into the breech. The weapon carried a spike bayonet. The need for a modern weapon set the Bavarian authorities a problem: the Prussian Dreyse had been issued to many German forces, but it was showing its age, especially compared to the French Chassepot. Adopted after trials the breech-loading Model 1869, the Werder rifle, was a different matter, designed to be simple in operation, one lever just forward of the trigger opened the breech, ejected the spent cartridge case and was ready to reload. It fired a metal cartridge with a calibre of 11.5mm and in the hands of a trained soldier was capable of firing 20–24 aimed shots in a minute. For good reason it was nicknamed the 'Blitz' or Lightning rifle! The sights could be adjusted to 1,200 metres. The Werder was issued with a slightly curved blade bayonet similar to the French *yatagan*.

Trousers were of the same blue material, with red piping down the outside seam. The *Jäger* battalions had the same uniform, but with green facings and piping and yellow metal buttons. They were also distinguished by the marksman award of green cord with two green pompons worn across the chest, a brass hunting horn badge on the cover of the pouch and a short green plume on the left side of the helmet. Each company in the infantry regiments had its 'sharpshooter' platoon, who wore their regimental colours with *Jäger* distinctions, green cords and pompons and brass hunting horn badge and green plume. Two types of footwear were worn: the standard German calf-length marching boots, and an older style with the shaft of the boot tightened by two buckles and straps. Officer's dress was similar, but with silver or gilt metal buttons and epaulette bridles. They did not wear a sash, but retained the gorget, which was covered in the same colour cloth as the tunic. All pack straps and belts were of black leather. At the rear of the belt was a single large ammunition pouch which could slide round to the side or the front of the body when in action. The belt had a simple brass buckle. On the left side a short sword and bayonet for the Podewils rifle was carried in black leather scabbards which were tied together with a narrow strap. Pack, mess tins and water-bottles were similar to the Prussia models. The greatcoat was generally strapped round the pack or rolled and carried over the shoulder. The greatcoat was made of black material, double-breasted with two rows of five yellow metal buttons, blue turn-down collar and deep cuffs. A small patch in the regimental colour was worn on the front of the collar. An off-white bread-bag was worn on the left hip.

From Napoleonic times Bavaria had stuck with its design of a leather helmet decorated with a woollen crest. Like the Prussian *pickelhaube* it had undergone some modifications and the model of 1845 had a reduced body formed from a single piece of leather to which was stitched a large front peak and a smaller rear peak. On the front was an ornate metal crowned 'L' (for King Ludwig II) and on each side a lion's face with a ring through its mouth from which hung a leather strap covered with metal scales and an adjustable buckle. On the top of the body was fixed a black padded woollen crest. On the left side, just above the lion fitting was attached a metal cockade painted with a white band, blue band and a white centre. It had a leather liner which could be adjusted to fit the wearer's head. The Model 1868 had a reduced height body, smaller front and back peaks and with a brass edging to the front peak. The front plate was the same as the Model 1845, as were the chin strap lions and cockade. The chin strap was leather with an adjustable buckle. Some of the earlier models had their brass chin scales removed and replaced with the Model 1868 strap. The black woollen crest was retained, as was the leather liner. On either side, next to the crest, was a small metal air vent. The officer's helmet crest was made from bearskin fur. The plate at the front was in two pieces: the 'L' and the crown. The silver and blue cockade had a smaller version of the crowned 'L' at its centre. As with most German leather helmets, the inside of the front peak was painted green and the back peak red.

The two cuirassier regiments wore the same uniform apart from the colour of the buttons: white metal for the 1st, yellow metal for the 2nd. Full dress was a cornflower blue single-breasted tunic with red collar and cuffs and piping down the front and on the rear skirts. It had white metal scale pattern epaulettes without fringes. The steel helmet had a high brass comb with a black horsehair crest and brass plate, edging to the peak, chin scales and fittings. A Bavarian cockade was on the left side above the chin scale boss. The cuirass was of steel with brass fittings. The trousers were blue piped red with thigh-length false leather boots. The pouch belt and sword belt were in white leather. In field dress the tunic was often replaced by a short waist-length stable jacket, called the 'spencer'. This item was the same blue as the tunic, but with only a red collar and red piping to the cuffs. Arms were a long straight sword and a muzzle-loading percussion pistol. The pistol ramrod was worn on a thin leather strap attached to the pouch belt. Officers wore the same uniform with either silvered or gilt metalwork and a narrow pouch belt covered in red leather. Horse furniture was a blue *shabraque* with red edging and a red crown in the corner, a blue portmanteau edged red with the regimental number at each end.

The six regiments of light dragoons all wore a deep-green double-breasted tunic with different facings and buttons: crimson for the 1st and 2nd; rose for the 3rd and 6th; and red for the 4th and 5th. The two rows of eight buttons were in white metal for the even numbered regiments and yellow metal for odd numbers. The facing colours were worn on the collar, cuffs and piping to the right front and rear skirts. White metal shoulder scales applied for all regiments. Green riding trousers were worn. The *spencer* was double-breasted with only the collar in the facing colour. The Model 1848 helmet was similar to the infantry Model 1848 with an additional two brass reinforcing strips on each side. All belts were white leather, with arms being a sabre and a percussion pistol. *Shabraques* had pointed corners and were green with edging and crown in the facing colour.

The two lancer regiments wore the same uniform of green double-breasted tunic with crimson collar, cuffs and piping, white metal buttons and white metal shoulder scales. The *spencer* was similar to that of the light dragoons. The lancer cap with its falling plume was worn in a black oilskin cover. It had a black leather peak and body with a crimson square top, all fittings in white metal and a black leather chin strap. The wooden lance had a white over blue pennon.

The Bavarian field artillery wore a similar style of uniform to the infantry, but the basic colour was a deep blue-black. The collar and cuffs were black with red piping with the piping also appearing down the front of the tunic and on the false pockets at the rear and down the outside seam of the trousers. The tunic had brass buttons and scale fringeless epaulettes. The trousers were tucked into the boots for the non-mounted men of the 3rd and 4th regiments, all other foot and mounted artillerymen had the leather-reinforced riding trousers. The artillerymen wore the Model 1848 helmet of the light dragoons, while officers and NCOs were issued with the new 1868 model. The helmet had a small red falling plume on the left side for mounted men and a small upright plume for the rest. The non-mounted men were armed with the infantry short sword, and mounted men with a sabre in a steel scabbard and white belts and staps. The *shabraques* were dark blue with red edging and crown. Officers had a pouch belt covered with black leather and a row of gilt buttons. Their sabres had a silver sword knot with a silver strap with two narrow blue lines. The engineers had the same uniform, but with white metal buttons and epaulettes, silver buttons for officers. They wore the infantry equipment and carried a carbine version of the Podewils rifle. All wore a short red plume on the helmet.

All Bavarian troops had a field cap in the colour of their tunic and piped round the base and crown in the tunic piping colour. It had a stiff leather peak and a black leather chinstrap. Officers had a metal crown and wreath on the front in the colour of the buttons, while other ranks had a yellow or white cloth crown.

The method of showing rank was unique to the Bavarian Army and consisted of lace edging bars worn on the collar in the button colour: one bar for a lance-corporal equivalent, lace edging and one bar for a corporal, sergeant edging and two bars, sergeant-major edging and three bars. Those of the officers were gold or silver depending on the button colour, second lieutenant one bar, lieutenant two bars, captain three bars. Those for major, lieutenant-colonel and colonel were the same with the addition of metallic edging. In addition, officers wore the gorget covered in tunic colour material. Staff officers had a sash in the Bavarian colours of silver with two blue lines. The Bavarian colours were a straight-sided, light blue *cross pattée* on a white field with the Bavarian coat of arms in the centre. In each corner was a crowned cypher in gold, either 'M' for King Maximilian or 'L' for King Ludwig.

6

Neutrals

Belgium

It was assumed by many that in the event of war between France and Prussia, an attack through Belgium by either side might reasonably be the first act, particularly after Emperor Napoleon III's attempt to annex Luxembourg in 1867. Indeed, in the early part of the war, French Marshal Canrobert brought his entire army corps (four infantry divisions) to Châlons-sur-Marne in northern France as a reserve and to guard against any Prussian advance through Belgium. When news of the declaration of war was received, the Belgian government of Jules d'Anethan (installed only two weeks before the war's outbreak), under King Leopold II, feared that it might be overrun. The gold reserves of the national bank were hurried to the National Redoubt at Antwerp (literally a last-ditch defence to which all available Belgian troops would retire to in case of invasion) before the news became public. When this leaked out, it caused panic.

The independence and neutrality of Belgium was guaranteed by a treaty dated 19 April 1839, which was signed by France, Prussia, Austria, Russia and England. On 9 and 11 August 1870, first France and then Prussia (which was now the Confederation of North Germany) and England re-signed the treaty reaffirming the independence and neutrality of Belgium and engaging to undertake a military intervention against one of the two belligerents should they invade Belgian territory.

The Belgian Army was called out on 15 July, the same day that both French and German armies mobilised. The Belgian troops were divided into two armies: the Army of Antwerp (15,000 men) and the Army of Observation (55,000 men) (see below).

Many Belgian military leaders feared that, even after the outbreak of hostilities, as both French and Prussian armies manoeuvred on the Belgian border, one of them would seek a strategic advantage by an outflanking attack through Belgium and most believed the army incapable of fending off any such attack. Despite key battles taking place very close to Belgian territory, including the Battle of Sedan just a few miles from the border, Belgium was never actually violated.

In order to avoid giving the impression of belligerence in the conflict, Leopold requested that the French not commit Belgian members of the French Foreign Legion during the conflict. The French agreed and Belgian Legionnaires remained in their base in French Algeria while their comrades were deployed to Metropolitan France.

From the beginning, the Belgian forces were divided into two armies: a mobile army called the 'Army of Observation' and the other garrisoning the military fortress of Antwerp. The commander-in-chief was King Leopold II, the Chief of Staff in day-to-day command was Lieutenant General Reynard. The Minister of War was another senior officer, Major General Guillaume. (General Reynard was Minister of War until

A Belgian border post in peace-time.

2 July 1870.) The Army of Observation was to monitor and protect the borders against any French or German intrusion and its movements were to follow those of the foreign armies along the Belgian border. The Treaty of 1838 that bound Belgium to neutrality, indicated that the first military force that entered the country should be regarded as an enemy.

The Army of Observation was commanded by Lieutenant General Baron Felix Chazal, a former Minister of War and of French origin. The Chief of Staff was Colonel Monoyer. It was composed of Ist and IInd Army Corps, artillery and cavalry reserve. The Ist Corps, commanded by Lieutenant General Fir, was composed of the first three divisions and a cavalry brigade. The IInd Corps, commanded by the brother of the King, HRH Philippe, Count of Flanders, was composed of the 4th and 5th Divisions and a brigade of cavalry. In addition, the army had engineering units, transport troops, telegraph operators and ambulances. The strength of this army was roughly 55,000 men.

The Army of Antwerp was grouped in the walled city itself. The entrenched camp was to become the ultimate fallback location of all the Belgian forces if severe setbacks forced a general retreat. The Army of Antwerp was commanded by Lieutenant General Eenens, with Colonel Brialmont as Chief of Staff. The forces were composed of the 6th Division and fortress troops. The strength of this army was roughly 15,000 men. Troops were also present in other fortified cities, including Liège, Namur, Ghent, Diest and Dendermonde (8,000 men).

The Belgian Army

By a law passed in 1868 the strength of the Belgian Army was fixed at 100,000 men on a war footing, and 40,000 in time of peace. It was formed by conscription, to which every able-bodied male was liable on completing his 19th year. Substitution, however, was permitted, and substitutes or volunteers actually formed a large part of the army. The annual contingent taken into the armed forces was 12,000 men. The period of service was eight years, of which two-thirds are passed on furlough.

The infantry consisted of one regiment of carabineers, three regiments of *chasseurs*, one regiment of grenadiers and 14 regiments of Line infantry. Each regiment had three field and one reserve battalion of four companies each, the latter in cadre only in peacetime. The cavalry consisted of four regiments of *chasseurs* and four regiments of lancers, each of four field and one depot squadron. The *chasseurs* formed on mobilisation the divisional cavalry, the lancers the reserve cavalry. The artillery was formed into four regiments and numbered 34 field and six reserve batteries of six guns each. The engineers were organised into one regiment of three battalions of four companies each, and five special companies comprising two telegraph, one railway and one pontoon as well as one of artificers. On mobilisation the Army formed two corps, each of two infantry divisions and a reserve of cavalry and artillery, and numbering 26 battalions, 16 squadrons and 96 guns.

As well as the standing army there was a civic militia (*Garde Nationale*), available for the defence of the country in time of war. This force, which numbered 125,000 men without the reserve and 400,000 men with the reserve, was formed of all citizens aged between 21 and 40 years of age who were able to bear arms but was only organised in the large towns and fortresses. In peacetime it was under the jurisdiction of the Ministry of the Interior, but in time of war under the Ministry of War.

The organisation of the Belgian Army was subjected to a practical test in 1870, when it was suddenly mobilised and placed in observation on the frontier. The results were not satisfactory. The actual numbers fell considerably short of the estimated ones, and of the men present a large number were quite unfit for service. The number of officers was altogether insufficient, and the Army was in many respects incompletely equipped. A bill for the reorganisation of the army, based on compulsory personal service, was introduced in 1871, and adopted in principle by an overwhelming majority of the commission appointed to examine it, but public opinion pronounced so decidedly against the abolition of substitution that the government gave way and the bill was withdrawn.

Bismarck's view of the Belgian Army, after some negotiations following the Battle of Sedan was not complimentary. He observed that the Belgian Army seemed to consist of a large amount of greatcoats and very little of soldiers!

Austria

After the defeat of the Imperial Royal Army in 1866, there was an enormous amount of discussion on what had happened and what should be done – but always within the constraint of the available funds. By 1870 some progress had been made. The Model 1867 Werndl breech-loading rifle system was adopted. The Conscription Act of 1868 made it mandatory for all males over 20 years of age to spend three years on military service (four years in the Navy). The cavalry had been reorganised with each branch having similar weapons, so that only the titles and uniforms differed. Tests were made of volley guns and mechanical machine guns, with the Gatling becoming the preferred choice. The most noticeable change was the disappearance of the traditional white coat and its replacement by a blue tunic.

Napoleon sent a general to Vienna in early July to coordinate a Franco–Austrian–Italian alliance with the south Germans (Bavaria) to invade Prussia. The stumbling block to Austria's (now Austria–Hungary) joining a French alliance, was of course, Bismarck. He had persuaded Russia that her best interests lay in friendship with Prussia and, in the event of Austria marching against Prussia in 1870, the Russian emperor was prepared to send 300,000 troops to Austrian Poland. Austria–Hungary, besides adopting a double name, had given the Hungarians their own government within the Hapsburg monarchy, which resulted in a separate cabinet and prime minister. The minister in the Austrian domains was keen to take revenge on

Prussia, but his counterpart in Hungary was committed to staying neutral in the conflict. The result was that no action was taken.

Denmark

Part of Napoleon's grand scheme was to send troops across the North Sea to Denmark and in conjunction with the Danish Army descend on Hamburg and Germany. What the Danes could get from this, apart from revenge, is difficult to see. The thought of re-occupying Schleswig and Holstein with their majority German populations would prove a nightmare and bring back all the problems that had beset the duchies for hundreds of years! Besides, Denmark was no longer the power she had been before 1864; she had lost the two richest and populous provinces of the kingdom and had resolved to reconsider her position in the world as one of the 'smaller kingdoms'. Its army, at full strength, stood at about 40,000 men and was barely a match for one Prussian Army corps and the reserves and *Landwehr* that could be mobilised against it.

England

On 9 August 1870 the British government signed a treaty with Prussia (the head of the North German Confederation) to agree the neutrality of Belgium and to undertake joint military action if the country was invaded by France during the current conflict. Two days later a treaty was signed between Great Britain and France on similar terms. What action could have been taken was not specified, but if either Prussia or France had operated on Belgian territory in defiance of the original treaty of 1839, which guaranteed the neutrality of Belgium, or the new treaty, Britain would have been obliged to cooperate with the other power to preserve Belgium's borders. It would have been interesting to see an Anglo–French military and/or naval force in Flanders, or an Anglo–Prussian army operating against the French. It could have altered the whole history of the late nineteenth and early twentieth centuries.

Bibliography and Further Reading (with Notes)

Some of the older books mentioned below are now difficult to find; however, it is worth searching the Internet for them as many have been scanned and made available in digital form.

Books

Adriance, Thomas J., *The Last Gaiter Button: A Study of the Mobilisation and Concentration of the French Army in the War of 1870* (Westport, CT: Praeger, 1987). ISBN: 0-313-25469-9. With reference to French archives, together with stories from French officers and officials, concentrates on the woeful inadequacies of French preparedness for war. Contains a very useful bibliography.

Barry, Quintin, *Moltke and His Generals: A Study in Leadership* (Solihull: Helion Books, 2015). ISBN: 978-1-910294-41-3. Contains character studies of leading German senior officers and members of the General Staff.

Borbstaedt, Colonel A. and Dwyer, Major F., *The Franco–German War to the Catastrophe of Sedan* (London: Asher & Co., 1873). Contains several chapters on the strengths, organisation and tactical formations of the French and German armies.

Colin, Commandant J.L.A., *The Transformations of War* (London: Hugh Rees Ltd., 1912). Translated by Brevet-Major L.H.R. Pope-Hennessy. Military thought with examples from an officer of the French *École de Guerre*.

Chapelle, Le Cte de la, *Les forces militaires de la France en 1870* (Paris: Amyot, 1872). Contains lists, tables of troops, organisations of all formations, weapons and so on of the French military in 1870. Text in French

Delpérier, Louis, *La Garde Impériale de Napoléon III* (Nantes: Éditions du Canonnier, 2000). ISBN: 2-912430-06-2. A lavishly illustrated tome with artwork and photographs of the uniforms of the Imperial Guard. Text in French.

Delpérier, Louis and Mirouze, Laurent, *The Franco–Prussian War 1870/71*, Volume 2 (Vienna: Verlag Militaria GmbH, 2020). ISBN 978-3-903341-04-3. Uniforms and equipment of the French armies. This is a companion book to Volume 1 on the German armies. Contains colour and black and white photographs of uniforms of the Imperial and Republican armies. Published in French, German and English versions. The English text can be a bit 'wobbly' in places.

Dumaine J. (publisher), *Description de l'Uniforme de l'Infanterie de ligne, des bataillons d'infanterie légère d'Afrique …* (Paris, 1868). Official regulations for the introduction of the new infantry uniform in 1868. French text plus line drawings.

Howard, Michael, *The Franco Prussian War* (London: Rupert Hart-Davis, 1961). ISBN 246 63587 8. Probably the best modern work on the war.

Horsetzky, General Adolf von, *A Short History of the Chief Campaigns in Europe since 1792* (London: J. Murray, 1909). As the title suggests, this is a brief account of the origins, plans, course and consequences of the war. The author was an Austrian corps commander and many of his comments are sympathetic to the Austrian armed forces.

Hozier, Captain H.M., *The Franco-Prussia War: Its Causes, Incidents and Consequences* (London: William Mackenzie, 1872). Contemporary standard work on the war. Hozier was with the Prussian forces, so his view of the proceedings was limited; however, he gives a detailed description of the organisation of both armies, based on *The Military Resources of Prussia and France* by Colonel Chesney and Henry Reeve, (1870), which itself was based on articles from *The Edinburgh Review* between 1864 and 1867.

Huon, Jean, *Les armes francais en 1870–1871* (Chaumont: Crepin-Leblond, 2007). ISBN: 978 2 70 300309 0. Handy illustrated reference guide to French and imported weapons. French text.

Huon, Jean, *Les armes allemandes en 1870–1871* (Chaumont; Crepin-Leblond, 2007). ISBN: 978 2 70 300307 6. As above but covering Prussian and Bavarian weapons. French text.

Jouineau, André and Mongin, Jean-Marie, *l'Armee de Napoleon III dans la Guerre de 1870* (Bayeux: Heimdal, 2018). ISBN: 978-2-84048-511-7. Words by Mongin, artwork by Jouineau, this contains 122 colour plates in the almost diagrammatic style used by Jouineau to illustrate uniforms and equipment of the French Army in the years leading up to 1870, including Guard, Line, North African troops, artillery, engineers, medical services, *Gardes Mobile* and *Franc-tireurs*. Text in French.

La Guerre Franco-Allemande 1870–1871: L'armement francais (*Gazette des armes* special issue, Paris 2001). Descriptions and full colour illustrations of French and imported small arms and edged weapons. French text.

Low, A.M., *Musket to Machine-gun* (London: Hutchinson, 1942). Compact wartime (Second World War) book describing the development of small arms from medieval to modern times (that is, the date of publication).

Moltke, Count Helmuth von, *The Franco–German War of 1870–1871* (London 1891). Translated by Clara Bell and Henry Fischer. The course of the war by the man himself. There is another version with slightly different text based on a 1907 publication and with a foreword by Michael Howard that was published London and California in 1992. ISBN 1-85367-131-2.

Newdigate, Colonel Edward (translator), *The Army of the North German Confederation … by a Prussian General* (London, 1872). Detailed descriptions of all branches of the Prussian Army and tactics used in the field.

Pietsch, Paul, *Formations und Uniformierungsgeschichte des preussischen Heeres 1808 bis 1914* (Hamburg: Helmut Gerhard Schultz, 1963). Two volumes: Volume 1 Foot troops; Volume 2 Mounted troops. Four colour plates and hundreds of detailed black and white line drawings in each volume. This is the 'bible' for German uniforms of the nineteenth century. German text.

Pratt, Edwin A., *The Rise of Rail-power in War and Conquest 1833–1914* (Philadelphia, PA/London: J.B. Lippincott Co., 1916). Contains interesting sidelights on the use of railways and the organisation of French and German railway troops.

Rousset, Lieutenant-Colonel L., *Histoire populaire de la guerre de 1870–71* (Paris: Quillet et Cie, n.d.). In two volumes with accounts of the war plus a large number of illustrations, mainly black and white, but some in colour by Maurice Pallandre as well as maps, plans and orders of battle. French text.

Stein, Markus and Bauer, Gerhard, *The Franco-Prussian War 1870/71*, Volume 1 (Vienna: Verlag Militaria GmbH, 2020). ISBN 978-3-903341-04-3. Details of uniforms and equipment of the German armies. Sumptuous volume of colour and black and white photographs covering Prussia, Brunswick, Saxony, Hesse, Baden, Württemberg and Bavaria. (See above for Volume 2 on France.) Original in German with versions translated into French and English, some of the English text is a bit 'odd'.

Stoffel, Baron, *Reports on the Military Forces of Prussia, 1868–1870* (London: Longmans, Green and Co., 1872). Stoffel was the French military attaché in Berlin appointed after the Austro–Prussian War.

Contains accurate insights into the Prussian military system and its superiority over the French, written between 1868 and 1870.

Stone, F. Captain Gleadowe, *Tactical Studies from the Franco–German War of 1870–71* (London: Kegan Paul, Trench & Co., 1886). Tactics of some of the early battles treated in detail, accompanied by excellent maps and plans, by an author who had walked the battlefields.

Sutherland, Stuart, *The Organization of the Army of the North German Confederation, 1870–1871* (Self-published by the author, 1995)

Sutherland, Stuart, *The German Navy of the Franco–Prussian War.* Articles in the *Foreign Correspondent* issues 52 and 55, the *Journal of the Continental Wars Society.*

Ullrich, Hans-Joachim, *Soldaten im Bunten Rock 3, Die preussische Armee 1840–1871* (Stuttgart: Franckh'sche Verlagshandlung, W. Keller & Co., 1970). Trilingual text (German, French and English) and folder with colour plates.

Wawro, Geoffrey, *The Franco–Prussian War: The German Conquest of France in 1870–1871* (Cambridge: Cambridge University Press, 2003). ISBN 0 521 58436 1. Lots of new research to add to Howard's narrative.

Newspapers

Illustrated London News, London, July–December 1870. Well-known for its excellent illustrations, based on drawings made on the spot by the paper's own staff and remade as woodcuts for publication. Also contains news items taken from the English press (notably *The Times* of London)

Illustrirte Zeitung, Leipzig, July 1870–June 1871. A weekly illustrated paper in German with excellent illustrations, same style as above.

Illustrirte Chronik, 'Wacht am Rhein', Leipzig, 1870–1871. Illustrated history of the war in two volumes. Some pictures similar to above. German 'Gothic' text.

L'Illustration, Journal Universal, Paris. French weekly illustrated newspaper. Many pictures from the French point of view. Text in French.